Wilson's Tales of the Borders
Historical, Traditionary and Imaginative
Revival Edition Volume 2

ISBN 978-0-9576187-6-3

Published by the Wilson's Tales Project, 2015.

The authors assert their moral right to be identified as the originators of their work within the publication and retain their own copyright.

All rights reserved. No part of this publication may be reproduced, stored in a retrieval system or transmitted, in any form or by any means, electronic, mechanical, photocopying, recording or otherwise, without the prior permission of the contributors.

Design by Morag Eaton

Edited by Joe Lang

Cover photograph by John Bryson: *The Monomaniac* in performance at Paxton House.

Printed in Berwick-upon-Tweed by Martins the Printers Limited
www.martins-the-printers.com

Contents

Introduction 4
The tale of Wilson's Tales 6
Tibby Fowler o' the Glen
    The Tale retold 11
    Background 19
The Faithful Wife
    The Tale retold 25
    Background 31
The Prisoner of War
    The Tale retold 39
    Background 45
The Surgeon's Tale: The Monomaniac
    The Tale retold 49
    Background 59
Launcelot Errington and his Nephew Mark: A Tale of Lindisferne
    The Tale retold 61
    Background 71
Hume and The Governor of Berwick
    The Tale retold 83
    Background 89
The contributors 94

Introduction

The Wilson's Tales Project started in 2013, to revive interest in both the Tales themselves and John Mackay Wilson, their original author.

Wilson's Tales of the Borders was a publishing sensation of the 19th century, launched by Wilson in Berwick-upon-Tweed when he was editor of the *Berwick Advertiser*.

One of the ways in which we have been reviving interest in the Tales has been to organise live events where artists retell them in contemporary ways for modern audiences. This work has been presented by professional storytellers, musicians singing ballads on which many of the Tales were based, local amateur dramatic groups performing new radio and stage plays, artists and film makers.

Our annual Revival Editions – of which this is the second – complement the live events, providing a more tangible presentation of the featured Tales for a wider audience to enjoy in their own time. We are concentrating on retelling these Tales and providing some background context to the times and events they depict. While some of the Tales may seem farfetched, and may at times stretch the truth of events, they often had real people and events at their core. They can tell us much about the lives, times and landscapes they portray.

This year's selection includes Tales of love and devotion – *Tibbie Fowler* and *The Faithful Wife* – set against backgrounds of war and hardship in the Borders that we now struggle to imagine.

The Adventures of Lancelot Errington and *Hume and the Governor of Berwick* are very much locally based. Lancelot Errington's Tale, set at the time of the Jacobite Rising of 1715, sounds like a completely ridiculous shaggy dog story but is essentially true. Hume was another larger-than-life local character: his Tale tells of a humorous – and successful – run-in with the rather pompous local authorities to win his love.

Later editions of the Tales drew on a wider canvas. They tell of Scots' adventures abroad – *The Prisoner of War* is set during the Napoleonic Wars and *The Monomaniac* centres on a voyage to India.

I hope you enjoy this selection. Next year we plan to introduce some entirely new Tales by including the three best entries from the short story competition held in local schools by our local Rotary Club.

If you'd like to find out more about the Tales, our events and what we are up to, please visit www.wilsonstales.co.uk and become a Follower to get regular emails.

Andrew Ayre

The tale of Wilson's Tales

Andrew Ayre begins a history of Wilson and his Tales with this account of how a century-long publishing phenomenon began.

Portrait of J M Wilson by James Sinclair.
Courtesy Berwick Museum and Art Gallery.

Wilson's Tales of the Borders and of Scotland, historical, traditional and imaginative are, as their compendious title suggests, a selection of stories, history and ballads principally relating to the Borders of Scotland and North Northumberland. This area was for many years known as the Debatable Lands: exactly where the border lay was a rather vague concept to those living there, as was the question of whether either Scots or English crown of the time had any real control over the area.

The Tales were first drawn together and published in weekly instalments from 8 November 1834 by John Mackay Wilson – at the time editor of the *Berwick Advertiser*. Publishing by weekly instalments was a common method used by, among others, Walter Scott and subsequently Charles Dickens.

Wilson was a Tweedmouth man who had a rather chequered career. He had tried to make a living in London through literary endeavours before returning to Berwick to take up what he hoped would be a more reliable salary as editor of the *Advertiser*.

When short of local news for the paper, he filled the spaces with some of his own work and local tales. These were well received. Spurred on by their success – and, no doubt, by suspicions that the son of the paper's proprietor was to be installed as editor on his return from university – Wilson decided to start publishing the Tales as a separate weekly publication for his own benefit.

In 1832 he had considered taking on the failing *Border Magazine* but decided against it. However, by 1834 he was ready to try his luck – no doubt noting that Walter Scott's death in 1832 had left a gap in the market.

As the subtitle suggests, the Tales themselves were a mixture of history, tradition and imagination. Many had their origins in Border ballads and the stories behind them.

Wilson was not the first to do this. James Hogg, the Ettrick shepherd, had in 1820 published *Winter Evening Tales* – made up largely from material previously published in his own short-lived magazine *The Spy*. He had also helped Walter Scott to gather many of the Scottish Border ballads published in *Minstrelsy of the Scottish Border* in 1802. Alan Cunningham, editor of the *London Magazine*, had published *Traditional Tales of the English and Scottish Peasantry* in 1822.

Wilson himself said, in a letter to a friend shortly before publication, that his intention was to compete with *Chambers Journal*. This was published from Edinburgh at the time and covered a wide variety of topics and stories.

He initially set out to publish 2,000 copies a week. But the Tales quickly became a publishing sensation: the print run was doubled three times in rapid succession, reaching 16,000 a week. Early editions had to be reprinted and within the first year plans were made to increase the run to 30,000 a week.

Weekly publications like this should perhaps be seen as the equivalent of today's soap operas. Families would keenly await the next edition – sitting down together on a Sunday evening to read the latest edition much as we would perhaps watch Downton Abbey. The Tales' original advertising and marketing emphasised their moral content, so that they would be acceptable reading on the Sabbath.

Sadly, Wilson was not to enjoy the fruits of his success. He died on 3 October 1835, less than a year after the first edition. By then he had contributed 66 Tales to the collection. His executors and family continued publication after his death to ensure his widow was not left penniless. They recruited new contributors – the first being Dr Alexander Allan Carr from Coldingham, who had just completed his *History of Coldingham*. One of the Tales he is thought to have contributed is *The Monomaniac*, on page 49 of this volume.

As the family quickly discovered, weekly publishing is a demanding task. They sold the publishing rights to John Sutherland of 12 Carlton Street, Edinburgh, the employer of one of Wilson's brothers. He recruited Alexander Leighton as the editor.

Leighton contributed many of the subsequent Tales himself and selected many more from a wide number submitted by aspiring authors. Under his editorship, publication continued for another five years with contributions from over 20 different writers.

In total 312 editions were published, including 485 Tales covering some 650 years of social history, heritage, lore and legend.

Newer contributors becoming involved in the project had limited knowledge of Border tales, and the scope of work broadened. *Wilson's Tales of the Borders* became *Wilson's Tales of the Borders and of Scotland*. The subject matter extended beyond Scotland to the adventures of Scotsmen abroad – prisoners of war in Napoleonic times, William Wallace attempting to gain support in France, young men adventuring and misadventuring in the West Indies and en route to India, and fur trappers enduring the hardships of Canadian winters.

The Tales portrayed not just heroes and heroines, but the lives of ordinary men and women. There were several series of 'tales within the Tales', including *The Lawyer's Tales, The Covenanters' Tales, The Minstrel's Tales* and so on.

With so many different contributors, there's an inevitable variety of styles – and indeed quality. The key to the Tales' enduring appeal and popularity was their subject matter, providing snapshots of history, events and circumstances that many could identify with.

The Tales written by Wilson himself are neat in their construction, interestingly expressed and generally very readable. Many later contributors were rather more prone to Victorian verbosity. Some of their Tales are written in strong Scottish dialect, spelled phonetically, which can be hard to follow even for Scots. As circulation became wider, complete editions were often published with a Glossary of the Scots Dialect. Many editions were taken abroad by emigrating Scots. These represented perhaps their most tangible connection with a homeland that many would not expect to see again.

The Tales remained immensely popular through the 1800s and were constantly reprinted. Over 40 different editions have been identified, including American, Australian and German versions.

A selection of Tales was published in 1934 as a single volume to celebrate the centenary of their first publication, and was republished in 1947. These editions give considerable background and would be recommended for a modern reader wanting further easy access to the Tales.

Andrew Ayre

# Tibby Fowler o' the Glen

Tibby Fowler o' the Glen **retold**

Tibby Fowler of the story and Tibbie Fowler of the well-known song share little but the name. Except perhaps a heap of gold – and a clutch of very suspect suitors!

In Wilson's story, Tibbie (he calls her Tibby) cuts a romantic and resourceful figure in a tale of rags and riches – while her namesake in song is portrayed as a proud and haughty flirt.

There are traces in land and history to which both characters have a claim, though 50 or more miles separate them. Both get an airing here, and you may make your own minds up… Maybe the song was written by one of those false lovers amidst the sour grapes of jealousy?

Tibbie Fowler o' the glen,
There's o'er mony wooin at her,
Tibbie Fowler o' the glen,
There's o'er mony wooin at her.
Wooin at her, pu'in at her,
Courtin at her, canna get her;
Filthy elf, it's for her pelf,
That a' the lads are wooin at her.
Ten cam east, and ten cam west,
Ten came rowin o'er the water;
Twa came down the lang dyke side,
There's twa and thirty wooin at her.
There's seven but, and seven ben,
Seven in the pantry wi' her;
Twenty head about the door,
There's ane and forty wooin at her.
She's got pendles in her lugs,
Cockle-shells wad set her better;
High-heel'd shoon and siller tags,
And a' the lads are wooin at her.
Be a lassie e'er sae black,
An she hae the name o' siller,

Set her upo' Tintock-tap,
The wind will blaw a man till her.
Be a lassie e'er sae fair,
An she want the pennie siller;
A lie may fell her in the air,
Before a man be even till her.
Wooin at her, pu'in at her,
Courtin at her, canna get her;
Filthy elf, it's for her pelf,
That a' the lads are wooin at her.

Though the song may be familiar, how many folk will be aware that 'the glen' itself is very near, not four miles from Berwick? Stretching beneath the grey ruin of Edrington Castle, the land forms a romantic amphitheatre where the Whiteadder coils serpentine and bright, glittering in the sun beneath the tumbled walls. Through the pastures it runs, below the crag topped by trees whose branches reach down to dabble in the winding river as it passes by.

If, by chance or curiosity, you should find yourself at this place, you will have with you the handiest of maps! You have only to stretch out your arm, and here at the shoulder sits Edrington Castle, while in the palm of your hand sits Clarabad. Near your elbow is the spot where 'ten cam rowing ow're the water' and next to it 'the lang dyke side' which cradles the site of Tibbie Fowler's cottage. And if the light falls in just the right place, you may see the shadow of a row of trees planted by Old Ned Fowler, Tibbie's father. Oh! He was a well-kent face in his own day, and time was that everyone hereabout knew this as the locality of the song, and often spoke of it. But as to the other particulars of the song, there remains a murky cloud of questions in which answers may be looked for, but not found.

This much at least is known: Tibbie's parents were a canny couple – 'Bein Bodies', as folks called them – and why not indeed? When her unfortunate mother and father passed away suddenly within a month or two of each other, they left their only child an orphan, bereft. However, they also left the sum of their own savings, plus a tidy legacy which had recently been bequeathed by a close relative. Put together, this left poor Tibbie in possession of £500. Yes! £500! Now, in these bygone days this was considered quite a considerable fortune.

And so Tibbie Fowler was left all alone in the world, the sole mistress of £500. Besides that, she inherited a neat, well furnished little cottage, not forgetting the land which the cottage sat in. All of this, and still she was only 19 years old.

But that's not the half of it! Wait till you hear how her hair was as black and glossy as a raven's wing glinting in the sunlight. Her face was as white as milk, kissed on each cheek with the hue of a rose. Her eyes glistened like dewdrops in a moonbeam and, to crown it all, her figure was so elegant and lovely that it could have made a glass eye weep!

Small wonder, then, that "all the lads cam' woo'in at her"! But, framed in beauty as she was, her heart was sensible and sober as a true woman's. All too soon, she found that her house was surrounded and her path beset by a herd of grovelling fellows, money-grabbers come to court her, and whose court she soon came to loathe. Of course they all said they adored her, they loved her, they would die for her. Yet mirrored on their eyeballs she saw money signs, and in their pleading sighs she heard whispers of: "Your gold, your gold, I want your gold"! In all truth, it was not that she really hated them, but she did despise their mean-minded and false intentions.

Finally, one by one, they gave up trying to win her, turned from her door in disgust and consoled themselves with spiteful words, inventing tittle-tattle, and generally predicting that 'pride comes before a fall'.

But it was not from pride that Tibbie rejected them. She was a sensitive soul and she knew that her heart was capable of real love: the devoted, pure and unchangeable love which grows with being beloved. In her heart of hearts she allowed that there may be some among these suitors whose motives were genuine, yet the whole gaggle of them together was too sordid to tell true from false. Above all, she knew that there was not one among them that made her heart flutter and none to whom her thoughts turned as a needle turns to a magnet by some mysterious, invisible force of nature. No, amidst this avaricious mob, she decided she would marry for herself – and that the man who won her hand would do so just for self only.

About a year after the sad loss of her mother and father, Tibbie sold her cottage and land, and off she went to Edinburgh Town to begin her life anew, where gossip of her being 'a great fortune' would no longer haunt her.

Now, adding to the numerous fine points already mentioned, Tibbie was the very prudent daughter of a very careful mother. Perhaps it would be too harsh to say every penny was a prisoner, but Mrs Fowler was certainly not in the habit of dipping her fingers into her savings without strong cause. Thus, imbued with her mother's homespun, frugal wisdom, the young woman went straightaway to deposit her money in what was then the capital's only bank. Next, she hired herself as a child's maid to the family of a gentleman living in the district of Restalrig. And so, soon, all that was known of Tibbie Fowler was that she possessed a kind, sweet nature and a very lovely face.

Sweet early summertime bloomed, and every day Tibbie took her young charges, one in her arms and the other by the hand, to stroll on Leith links. Here she could wander slowly by the sound of the sea, which roused in her sweet memories of her parents, of home, and the sound of the deep waters rushing through the fairy glen. Those who have grown up by the sea often remark that the swell of the tide is familiar and comforting as an old friend; and so it was for her, recalling her happy childhood in the glen.

Tibbie had only been with her new family for a few weeks when, returning from her daily walk, she happened to pass a young man dressed in seaman's clothes. Now, it was only the merest of glances – but she registered that he was around 25 years, or thereabouts, and though he wasn't exactly handsome, his features were strong, rugged and with a dash of bold confidence in his eyes. As their eyes met in the flicker of a moment, he turned aside as if embarrassed, and moved swiftly on.

How Tibbie's heart jumped! She blushed; then, feeling foolish at blushing, blushed even deeper, although her footstep never faltered. For she had seen something in his gaze that she had never seen before, she felt as she had never felt before, and she had to check her instinctive wish to turn around, which caused her to blush all over again!

On she strolled, obeying modesty rather than curiosity, until the wee laddie at her side began to fall behind and she was obliged to look back and call him by name. Admittedly, she may have looked at the spot where the sailor had been – but only by the merest coincidence or motiveless accident, she was sure. In any event, the sailor had changed direction and was now following her at some distance, and continued to do so all the way back to her master's door. She knew, because she could hear his footsteps behind her.

Well, at first Tibbie wasn't quite sure if she was pleased or annoyed by his following her. But no doubt you will guess which feeling was the stronger. The next day he was there again, and the next, and the next, following always at some distance. How long this arms-length courtship continued I can't tell you. But what I can be sure of is that they spoke, he wooed, and around a year later, Tibbie Fowler became the beautiful blushing bride of one William Gordon, first mate of a foreign trader.

Not two weeks after their joyful wedding, William was due to set off on a long voyage which was expected to last around a twelvemonth. It is no surprise that the young bride could not bear the thought of being parted so long from her darling husband – who was as yet ignorant of her dowry. Just a few days before the marriage she had removed the money from the bank and put it in her own safe-chest, ready for the right time to tell him of the secret fortune; and that time had come.

"Oh Wullie, my ain dear Wullie," she pleaded, "ye canna gang frae me already! I've neither faither, mither, brother nor sister, only you, dearest, in the whole wide world! Dinna leave me on ma ain!" And she wrung his hand, gazed imploringly into his eyes and wept.

"Dearest, I maun gang, you know it", said Wullie, hugging her close "but the months will race away like shadows chased by moonlicht owr'e the sea! It's an easy voyage, hinny – nae danger at all – an' oh, dinna greet!" he begged, wiping away her tears. "For when I come back I'll make ye the fine leddy o' them a'!"

"Oh no, Wullie, I want to be nae leddy! I just want to be wi' you," she said resolutely. "You wait here, for there's somethin' I have to show ye". And she hurried to her wooden chest and pulled out a large leather pocket book that had been her father's, and which contained her treasure – now amounting to around £600. She pressed it to her husband's chest and whispered, "There, dearest, that is yours now. My faither gave it to me with his blessing, and so do I to you with mine, only dinna, dinna leave me!" And with that she turned and hurried out of the room.

Now, you may imagine the amazement and joy of the fond husband on opening the pocket book and finding the unlooked-for fortune! All thoughts of leaving his dear wife for a long voyage were immediately wiped away. Instead, with her blessing, he purchased a small coasting vessel and so became both owner and commander.

The next few years were ones of unclouded prosperity and joy, in which Tibbie became the adoring mother of three fine children. Wullie sold the small vessel, and bought a larger one, which, after fitting it up, swallowed all the profits of the last five years. But, no matter! Trade was grand and she was a beautiful brig, which Wullie proudly called the Tibbie Fowler. Soon it was time to set off on a short foreign trip of about four months, which he expected to be very advantageous.

Four long months went by slowly enough. Then six, eight, 10 and 12 months dragged by in which the distraught wife heard no word at all of her dearest man nor the bonny ship. These were dangerous times to roam the seas, for Britain was at war and the oceans were ploughed by enemy ships and pirates. To make matters even worse, there had been fierce storms and wild hurricanes since Wullie had set sail.

Poor Tibbie dwelt on these horrors and wept to herself. Her children constantly asked for Daddy, who had gone away so very long ago. He had promised, after all, that he would bring presents when he came home. When was Daddy coming home? When? Tibbie could only say, "Tomorrow, dears, maybe tomorrow," then turn to hide her tears.

Eventually her money ran out. The friends of their prosperity helped at first, but as all hope of his return faded, and what with the brig not being insured, finally she and her children were reduced to beggary. Tibbie sold one piece of furniture after another until what was left was seized by the landlord in place of the rent. Then the mother and her young children were put out on the streets with scarcely a blanket to their name, to beg – or worse – or die. From the remnants of her friends, she got a basket and a few bits and pieces to sell; and so, broken-hearted and full of grief, Tibbie set out with her children, wandering from village to village.

Weeks dragged into months, until she drew close to the glen where she had been born, drawn by a desperate longing to see her old home one more time. At last she stood in that place so familiar. There was the dyke, the trees, the water, as in a dream. But she and her family were bone weary and desperate, starving, her children wailing, as in that cold dream Tibbie rushed forward to her old front door and hammered on it with her fists. The door was opened by a familiar face – a man who had, all those years ago, been one of the sullen gold-diggers she had rejected. Now he looked down upon her with narrowing, scornful eyes.

"Well, well, well!" he said, looking her up and down "If it isn't Tibbie Fowler!" Even in her wretchedness she was still a beauty. "Ye poor creature! Is it charity yer after? Ha! D'ye mind when I said pride would come before the fall?"

But before the last cruel words were out of his mouth he was pushed aside.

"Tibbie, my ain Tibbie! Oh, ma bairns!" And there, catching her up in his arms was William Gordon, her long lost husband! Now what joy, gratitude and unspeakable relief flowed between them! Only three weeks before, he had landed on British shores, and he had tramped the country over looking for her, tracing her from village to village until here, like a miracle, he found her on her very own old doorstep.

Wullie's story is too long to tell you here, but in short he had fallen into enemy hands. Then he had been enslaved on their ship and his own vessel commandeered until, in a raging storm of monstrous ferocity, by his own strength and skill he saved both ship and crew from a watery grave. In gratitude for their lives, the pirates gave him his liberty, returned to him his own ship, and he landed home 18 months after he first set sail, far richer, and laden with honours!

There is little enough left to tell. After recovering from the shock and delight of being reunited, the family left that place and once again prospered in great joy and contentment. After a few more years, Wullie and Tibbie bought back the cottage in the glen and settled there. Tibbie Fowler lived to see her grandchildren thrive, and when she died, it was at a great age in the very house in which she had been born – the shadows of which you may trace in the landscape of the glen till this very day!

Retold by **Mary Kenny**

Background to *Tibby Fowler o' the Glen*

Tibby Fowler is one of Wilson's own stories, one he may have heard first-hand. The story has a local setting on the northern bank of the River Whiteadder near Berwick, moves to Edinburgh and returns to Berwick.

In his introduction, Wilson equates Tibbie (or Tibby, as he spells her) with the Tibbie Fowler featured in an old song. This is sometimes attributed to Robert Burns but is actually much older: as with many of his songs, Burns polished-up an existing folk song. Allan Ramsay mentions it as the tune to one of his own songs.

> *Tibbie Fowler o' the glen*
> *There's o'er mony wooin at her*
> *Tibbie Fowler o' the glen*
> *There's o'er mony wooin at her.*

Wilson's story has Tibbie orphaned at the age of 19 and beset by suitors, all after her inheritance of £500. She sets off to Edinburgh to work as a nanny to "a gentleman in Restalrig" – keeping her tocher, or dowry money, a secret so that she will no longer be wooed by false swains.

The mention of Restalrig may be significant in unravelling Tibbie's identity.

Wilson gives explicit details of where Ned Fowler, Tibbie's father, had his cottage and smallholding. It stood above a small glen on the north side of the Whiteadder, four miles west of Berwick-upon-Tweed.

Despite the rain, the glaur and the clart, I tramped off to find Tibbie's cottage – or at least the spot where, according to Wilson, it stood between Edrington Castle and Clarabad. The glen, now densely wooded, is home only to roe deer and buzzard, with ancient moss and lichen-covered trees and new plantings. The farmer soon put me right as to the site – still marked on farm maps as Tibbie's Cottage on a promontory above the river, and apparently once the location of an Iron Age fort.

The little bridge nearby is called Tibbie's Bridge and the field is called Tibbie's Field; but of her dwelling, not a stick or stone remains.

There are the decaying trunks of mighty elms, long since cut down, around the edge above the steep drop to the river. Are they the remnants of the trees planted by Ned Fowler, surely misprinted as 'palms' in Wilson's tale: "...a shadowy row of palm trees (sic) planted by the hand of Tibbie's father – Ned Fowler"?

The Tibbie Fowler of the story seems to have been a real person. In the tale, she marries a sailor, William Gordon: they buy a brig with her dowry and prosper in the coastal trade until he is captured by enemy ships and disappears for 18 months. Tibbie and her children are reduced to destitution until William returns laden with riches and honours and they settle down in her father's old cottage. It's a fairly typical Wilson tale.

But Wilson's Tibbie is a great beauty with cheeks "where the lily and the rose have lent their hue". The song makes it clear that the attraction of its Tibbie is her wealth, not her looks. She has jewels in her ears and silver-strapped high-heeled shoes:

She's got pendles in her lugs…
High heeled shoon and siller
tags

Not at all like the douce Tibbie of Wilson's tale.

The cynical, worldly humour of the song is also found in

Isabella (Tibbie), daughter of Captain Ludovic Fowler, married George Logan of Restalrig in June 1640. This is her wedding dress - worn by a descendant of George's, Jean Logan, in 1933. Picture courtesy of Caroline Faed, Tibbie's eight-times-granddaughter.

Allan Ramsay's *Gie me a lass wi' a lump o' land* and Burns' *Hey for a lass wi' a tocher*. Both imply that beauty doesn't last but wealth does. *Kate Dalrymple* has a similar theme.

These are not the sentiments of romance and virtue rewarded that suffuse Wilson's Tales. I think Wilson has conflated two different stories and two very different Tibbies.

For the Tibbie of the song I would have to look further afield. And Restalrig might be a clue: why did Wilson mention that specific part of Edinburgh? I went to seek some answers in our capital city.

> *Tibbie Fowler o' the glen, there's ower mony wooin' at her*
> *Wooin' at her, pu'in at her*
> *Wantin' her, canna get her*
> *Silly elf, it's for her pelf*
> *A' the lads are wooin' at her*

The Logan family had a long history of association with the Scottish Crown. A Logan had accompanied the 'Good Sir James' Douglas on his ill-fated mission to the Holy Land with Bruce's heart. By 1382 the Barony of Leith had come into their possession.

Good and bad, they ruled over the port and the neighbouring estate of Restalrig until the early 16th century – by which time the lands had been divided among three branches of the family. Sir James Logan, Sheriff or 'Shirra' of Edinburgh, built his mansion where St Thomas' church stands at the top of Sheriff Brae. The church is now a Sikh temple.

The catastrophe of Flodden and subsequent, ill-judged political ventures brought a decline in Logan fortunes until, in the late 16th century, Robert Logan – "ane godles, drunkin and deboshit man" – had lost his Restalrig lands to pay his debts. After his death, he was accused of involvement in the Gowrie conspiracy; the family were outlawed and any remaining lands confiscated.

Eventually, some of their lands in Berwickshire were returned to them and the sentence of outlawry revoked. Respectability of a sort returned to the family. Tradition has it that George Logan, a grandson of Robert, married "weel tochered" Isabella Fowler and, with her large dowry, built a mansion at the head of Shirra Brae where he could view all the comings and goings of Leith Harbour.

Isabella was the daughter of Ludovic Fowler of Burncastle near Lauder. Burn Castle stood overlooking the Earnscleugh Water, near one of the branches of the ancient Herring Road winding its way from Dunbar to Lauder. Of the castle, nothing remains except the name of the farm on the site.

Another version has her as the daughter of a portioner, or owner of a small portion of land, at Lochend – now a sprawling housing estate. Lochend House, built in 1820, incorporates the gable end of the old Logan stronghold, Lochend Castle. I think this is less likely, given the amount of money needed to restore the Logan fortunes and rebuild on the old site of Shirra House.

It seems to be the old story of the nouveaux riches buying their way into an ancient family name. One can imagine the folk of Leith, who had not always benefited from their Logan superiors, having a good laugh in the taverns along the shore as the wags sang their comic songs about the newest lady of the house with her jewels and high-heeled shoes and attempts to overcome the deficits of nature.

> *She's got pendles in her lugs, aye cockle shells would set her better*
> *High-heeled sheen wi' siller tags and a' the lads are wooin' at her*

This must be the Tibbie of the satirical song.

Wilson's bonny Tibbie Fowler's £600 might have bought a coastal trading boat. But even in those far-off times it wouldn't have been enough to build the mansion house in Leith and pay off the Logan debts. It is also unlikely that a smallholder at Lochend would have accumulated enough of the "penny siller" to make George Logan throw his hat into the ring with the other suitors.

> *Ten cam' east and ten cam' west and ten cam' sailin' ower the water*
> *Twa cam' doon yon lang dyke side, there's ower mony wooin' at her*

No, for my money, and for Tibbie's, it has to be Isabella Fowler of Burncastle.

Wilson seems to have conflated the local story of Tibbie Fowler of the Glen – a charming, pretty young woman of comfortable means – with an earlier tale of the rich, aristocratic if less than beautiful heiress, Tibbie Fowler of Burncastle. When he attached the old song to his tale, he completely overlooked its satirical overtones.

Background by **Dr Michael A Fenty**

The Faithful Wife

The Faithful Wife retold

Just over 500 years ago, the Battle of Flodden was a disaster for the Scots. The shock defeat of their numerically superior army cost them their king and much of their nobility. Historians typically tell the story from the perspective of monarchs and generals. By contrast, The Faithful Wife focuses on an ordinary footsoldier – and his wife.

The Flodden Memorial Cross. Photograph by Dr Chris Burgess.

As Alexander Hume walked up Selkirk High Street on his way home, he looked in the window of the candlestick maker's shop. It wasn't open. No one was in. Normally, this shop provided light. Now, the darkness inside allowed him to see his reflection in the window, and the rest of the street behind him. Nowhere was open. No one was in. No one was walking about. He'd lost track of what day or time it was, but there was daylight and he was sure it was still September. Selkirk was normally heaving during the harvest season.

Where was Mitchy the candlestick maker? Where were all the other small business owners? Normally people would have their shops open during the harvest season, as the town would be thronging and business would be lively. But the town wasn't thronging and business wasn't lively.

Alexander's own business, his smithy, was just a while north of the town, past John Dawes' farm. Alexander continued along the horse track between two of John's fields. By now his armour really was getting heavy again. He wished he'd made it thinner, out of a lighter metal. Then he looked down and saw the gash of an English billhook close to his heart and was glad he hadn't. If only more of the men had bought his new armour, he thought. They'd said it was too expensive, he was asking too much money for it; and for many he had seen, that had been a costly decision.

So much carnage! He had seen Agnew slain in the distance, the blade of a bill to his neck. Hamish had fallen by his side, the point rupturing his armour from rival Fairbairn's smithy. Had Alexander been wrong? Was it all his fault? If he hadn't wanted so much for the new armour, would these men not have died? But Alexander now had three mouths to feed. His wife had recently given birth to their first child, Patrick. The birth was unplanned, though not unwanted; but Alexander had to do what he could to feed the wife and baby, and keep them warm.

And would the armour have made that much of a difference? So many trampled. The Scots had charged down Branxton Hill, the ground wet underfoot. Their powder had been wet and the angle of their cannons down the hill towards the English meant the cannon balls were rolling out down the hill, spreading the King's own men like skittles or dominoes. Men would fall but the charge would continue, "fer Croon and Country". The men had charged. And for Croon and Country they would die. As they approached the English billmen their pikes were too long and cumbersome. They were cast away. As the Scots drew their swords they were parried away by the English billmen. Then another billhook would pierce their calf and tear them asunder. As these men lay on the floor, there was no time to rescue the wounded. The English were too close and their bills too long. These men were trampled by the oncoming Scots, charging to their doom. It was a bloodbath. As the red sky had drawn in towards the setting sun, Alexander had felt choked by the oozing stench of liquid death.

Now the smell was different. He could smell the harvest, bluebirds were singing and the wheat, maize and oilseed rape were being gathered in. Wasn't it a bit late to be bringing in the harvest? Those crops should be on the market by now. Alexander looked closer. It was hard to make out the people collecting the barley. These weren't the shapes of, big strong men in the distance. Why were the women and children so involved with the harvest? Had John, so obsessed with preparing for the battle, left it so late to bring the harvest in that he now had all hands on deck to get it done in time? John. John had ordered himself a new helmet, sword and breastplate the moment the battle was announced, and Alexander had worked tirelessly to get them made in time. John could often be seen out practising with wooden alternatives while he waited.

Another memory of the battle came back to Alexander. He had seen a breastplate like the one he made for John, face down in the dirt. He hadn't been certain it was one and the same at the time, his face awash with blood, the tears, sweat and gore rushing past his eyes and sometimes into his mouth and nostrils. The face of the corpse was unrecognisable for the carnage caused to it by the English ferocity. But now Alexander was certain. He had sculpted that breastplate himself and there was no other like it. John Dawes was dead. What a terrible business! Hume had seen so many fall on Flodden field and couldn't remember all who died, or be sure that any were in fact alive. Was this why nowhere was open, and the women and children worked the fields?

It dawned on Alexander that there were, simply, no men left. He'd not seen any man alive on his journey back from Branxton. All gone, all gone, all dead. A tear ran down his face again and he hurried his pace to get back to his missus. Margaret may be the only wench in the town with her man coming back to her, and she needed him now more than ever. She still had the newborn young man to feed. And if the harvest hadn't been taken in, this would be a monumental task.

Alexander felt that after showing his wife he was safe and well, it was his duty to join in with the harvest, to help the women and children. He didn't know how to do it, but he couldn't bear to forge another sword, item of war or harbinger of death. He would become a farmer and provide for his family – and for the many widows and orphans of his town. This was his purpose. This was why the Lord had sent an angel with a white feather in its helmet to defend him whenever his battle seemed over.

This courageous soldier had been there for Alexander throughout the battle. Whenever he advanced into the English line, wreaking havoc and exposing himself to an opportunistic billman, the soldier with the white feather had come in to pluck the billman's life away. Alexander had been grateful for this wingman, allowing him to fight the battle as aggressively as he knew how, always with someone to watch his back. Alexander had asked for the soldier's name and even offered to buy him a drink in quieter, more peaceful times if both survived. He hoped this man had survived. More so than any of his friends from Selkirk, Alexander hoped that this man with the white feather in his helm had survived, for not one other person had shown such loyalty in years of friendship as this one man in a few hours of battle. Yet Alexander could have sworn they hadn't met before.

Alexander's pace quickened. He couldn't wait to get back to his wife and child and tell them of his saviour's brave deeds. His wife, Margaret, had not wanted him to go to the war. She had pleaded with him to stay, not to give up his life for another man's cause, to think of their newly born son and how much he needed a father. This wasn't like when Alexander used to go on the border raids when he was younger. Now he had responsibility and mouths to feed. He couldn't go throwing away his life to earn the favour of the French queen for a king he'd never met.

"But every man in the village will be fighting side by side, for Croon and for Country. I cannae not go. It'll bring shame on us, shame on the family, shame on the great Hume clan."

"Is the only thing you can think of your pride? What about your wife, your child? Do they matter not?"

"It is not my decision. King James has made his choice. We go to war." Those were the last words Alexander spoke to Margaret before he left, on the eve of battle. He couldn't believe he had left her on such bad terms. What if he had died in the battle? Would that be his loving wife's last memory of him, one of anger? Fear not, thought Alexander, for I have survived. I, unlike so many, will have the chance to make amends. Despite this bittersweet feeling, Alexander thanked the Lord that he was alive, and almost forced a smile as he knocked on the door of his cottage. Margaret had always admired his smile, and if she were to have a lasting image of him he would want it to be his grin.

There was no answer. Alexander knocked again. Still no answer. He carefully prised the door open.

No one came to meet him. No sound, either of wife or child, met his ear. On looking round he saw, sitting in an armchair, the person who had accompanied him in battle, wearing the same haubergeon, the same helmet, the individual white feather that had attracted his attention. That person was Margaret Hume. She was dead. Her head reclined on the back of the chair, her arms hung by her side, the edge of her haubergeon was uplifted, and at her white bosom, from which flowed streams of blood, her child sucked the milk of a dead mother.

Alexander's tears welled up. He let out a cry in anguish and fell to his knees. He struggled across the floor to remove the feathered helmet and put a hand on his wife's face. No pulse as it coldly, blankly stared back at him. Alexander drew his blade and pressed it to his stomach. He was about to push the blade in to his flesh and join his wife and all the other men of Selkirk in the afterlife.

Then he heard a breath. Breathing. It couldn't be his wife: he put his ear to her mouth and felt nothing. He looked down — the breathing was coming from the child. His son was still alive. Who was Alexander to kill himself and leave the newborn to fend for itself? Although his child would have to become a man, and quick. Because there were none left. Not only did the child need Alexander, but so did the rest of the town. Alexander put away his blade. He, his son and the remaining women and children would need to rebuild Selkirk.

Retold by **David Ayre**

Background to *The Faithful Wife*

Wilson's Tales were subtitled as being 'historical, traditionary and imaginative'. *The Faithful Wife* is typical in offering a mix of all three – with history and tradition as a background to imaginative storytelling.

The Battle of Flodden certainly happened. It was a bloody and brutal clash between the Scots and the English to the north of Wooler outside the village of Branxton on 9 September 1513. It is still very much remembered locally: a riding-out to the battlefield from Coldstream is held every year, with a rather moving service of remembrance for the fallen at the battlefield. A granite cross, erected in 1910, marks the battlefield site and there is a more recent interactive Battlefield Trail.

The opposing monarchs were James IV of Scotland and his brother-in-law Henry VIII of England. There had been peace between the two nations and rival kings for some years beforehand; but it was a rather uneasy peace.

The Scots had attacked Norham in 1497 with Mons Meg, the famous cannon now at Edinburgh Castle. This was followed in 1497 by the Truce of Ayton and in 1502, as part of the marriage contract between James IV and Margaret Tudor, a Treaty of Perpetual Peace. This didn't last long. James effectively broke it when he crossed into England in the lead-up to Flodden.

James IV was arguably one of Scotland's greatest kings. He had done much to unite the country as a kingdom, finally bringing some of the wilder and more lawless edges of the country in the Western Highlands and Isles and the Scottish Borders under the control of the central monarchy.

He saw himself as a somewhat heroic, knightly character and seemed to need little encouragement to further his ambition and consolidate his reputation.

In 1513, Henry VIII revived the ancient English claim to the French throne and led an English army to invade northern France. James was now caught between two mutually exclusive treaties: the Treaty of Perpetual Peace with England and the long-standing Auld Alliance with France.

In the summer of 1513 – egged-on by the French, who were keen to open up a second front against England, and irked by ongoing disputes such as Henry's reluctance to pay-over his wife's legacy – James crossed into England with the largest army ever assembled in Scotland.

Henry was engaged fighting in France. So he sent Thomas Howard, Earl of Surrey, north to address the Scots invasion with such troops as he could muster.

On paper Flodden was a battle that the Scots should never have lost. King James, aged 40, was in his prime. He led a Scots army of 40,000 men, perhaps more – outnumbering the English army at least two to one. The French had supplied him with the latest weapon of war, the long pike. And he held a commanding position on Flodden Hill.

But the wily Earl of Surrey, then in his 70s, was experienced enough to appreciate his disadvantages. Arriving at the southern end of Glendale Plain, he declined to meet James in battle on the flat ground and realised the futility of a frontal assault, knowing both options were futile. Instead, he headed off towards Berwick.

The Scots may have thought he was abandoning any thought of confronting them. He wasn't. At a stroke, the whole strategic position changed. The Scots on their commanding hill were outflanked. Surrey, if he wished, was now in a position to cross the Tweed at Berwick and march unimpeded to Edinburgh. James was in danger of swapping his capital city for a small hill in Northumberland.

In the event, Surrey crossed the Till at Weetwood Bridge and recrossed it at Twizel Bridge (both bridges still exist), outflanking the Scots to appear behind them on a slightly lower hill to the north of Branxton.

When battle was engaged, the English were able to bring their cannon and archers into effective play. The Scottish artillery was facing the wrong way and couldn't be repositioned and lowered quickly.

On the western flank, Borderers featured on both sides of the battle. They seemed remarkably reluctant to fight one another, perhaps recognising that blood feuds would last much longer than a quarrel between distant kings.

Fatally, James decided to take the battle to the English. Why? Boldness or impatience, perhaps; or he may have felt disadvantaged by the long-distance engagement, in which he could not bring his numerical superiority into play.

Whatever his reasoning, the central part of the Scottish army descended from its hilltop to engage with the English army, poised on the adjoining hill. But James had not allowed for the bogginess of the ground in between. The Earl of Surrey, waiting patiently, had perhaps foreseen this.

The French pikes were 15-18 feet long and unwieldy, particularly in inexperienced hands. They could really only be used effectively if a tight phalanx formation of bristling weaponry was maintained. By the time the Scots got through the mud and started heading up the other side, what order they had was broken and they were weighed down by water and mud. Their move had also given the English the advantage of the higher ground. The English archers' arrows rained down; then the English pikemen, with their billhooks, found it comparatively easy to cut the dangerous ends off the Scots' pikes.

James himself, determined to save the day, made matters worse by ploughing into the melee with most of his loyal supporters. All oversight, perspective or control over the battle and troops was effectively lost.

On the eastern flank the English gained a decisive victory, leaving James no chance of rescue. The Scottish side was largely made up of Highlanders, more used to skirmishes and guerrilla warfare than pitched battles. Poorly equipped and armoured for the task, they were quickly driven back – then caught in a devastating attack from the late-arriving Sir Edward Stanley's longbowmen.

Now outflanked by the English army on both sides, upwards of 10,000 Scots lost their lives in the slaughter that followed – including the King and much of the Scottish nobility. English losses numbered perhaps a few thousand.

To this day, Flodden is seen as a resounding Scottish defeat. But while England claimed victory on the day, the Scots won later battles to defend the Borders.

They had lost their King and much of their nobility – a desirable or undesirable outcome, depending on your political persuasion. But there would undoubtedly have been a significant number of angry Scots around the next day. And the remaining Scottish army would still have outnumbered the English two to one.

However, under the leadership of Lord Home the Scots held back. Rather than pursue the English, Home opted to work with the remaining Scottish forces and barons to secure the border and Scottish defences. This proved a successful strategy.

The English army largely disbanded, and the Earl of Surrey headed south to claim political credit for victory, leaving a relatively small force in place.

Although his army outnumbered the English at Flodden, James had made a major miscalculation in that the population of England was five times that of Scotland: so raising additional armies was a relatively simple task. Two more English armies had been moving north to counter the Scots. One was led by Catherine of Aragon, who by 9 September had reached Buckingham with a growing force of 14,000. Another force, at Leicester, was already 40,000 strong.

The Scots were now defenders rather than aggressors, and the citizens of Edinburgh lost no time in building the 'Flodden Wall' in case of attack. In the next engagement, when English forces tried to cross the border on 13 November, they were roundly defeated.

By the following year, King Henry's agents were complaining that Scottish raiders were once more making incursions across the border into Northumberland with virtual impunity.

The Borders warlords, known as reivers, had long preferred a weak Scottish king. Now they were pretty much left to do as they wished; within a year they seemed to be very much back to business as usual. The squabbling around the regency of the infant James V allowed them more licence to behave as they chose.

Flodden was probably largely removed from English history because the victory belonged officially to Catherine of Aragon, whom Henry divorced. How this must have hacked Henry off! Flodden was the most significant military victory of his reign, and he did not get the credit.

It was many years – indeed centuries – later that Flodden came to assume greater significance. In the 18th century – as again in recent years – ancient conflicts between 'noble Scots' and 'wicked English' were revived as part of the PR battle between pro and anti union parties.

The century began with the 1706 and 1707 Acts of Union abolishing the Scottish Parliament to create the United Kingdom under one Westminster Parliament; and it saw a period of rebellion and Jacobite uprisings before the final 1800 Act of Union which gave us, amongst other things, the Union Jack.

The introduction to *The Faithful Wife* refers to Selkirk's coat of arms, depicting a woman with babe in arms above the Scottish saltire. Its origin, we are told, lies in the exploits of Alexander Hume and his wife Margaret, recounted in the Tale. The emblem can certainly be found in Selkirk, most notably in stained glass at the Church of Our Lady and St Joseph. There was another at a church in the depths of the Ettrick Forrest which has now gone. It is used as part of the town trail and on the banner for the Riding of the Bounds. To the uninformed eye, the image looks as much like the Madonna and child as a survivor from Flodden, so one can take one's pick as to whether this Tale is more historical or imaginative.

Selkirk's main Flodden-related legend is represented by the Fletcher Monument in the town square. This features a wounded warrior holding a flag aloft. Tradition holds that Fletcher was the only man to return to Selkirk from the 80 who left for battle; but local historian Walter Elliot has found little support for this in the Selkirk archives.

The Fletcher Monument, Selkirk. Photograph by John Bryson.

In the town's Burgh Court books, the only reference to Flodden is a case where someone accused of stealing a horse claimed to have acquired it from the battlefield. There was no record of land passing to heirs, which might have been expected after such slaughter – though perhaps it was the heirs themselves, rather than their fathers, who failed to return?

In fact, there's little mention of Flodden in the written record until the 1700s. The first accounts suggesting that it was a great disaster appeared only in 1722, and the first reference in Selkirk itself was in 1790.

From a literary perspective, Walter Scott's poem *Marmion* – published in 1808, not long before the first Wilson's Tales appeared – conjured up a highly romanticised version of events.

More recently, the battle's 500th anniversary in 2013 prompted a number of publications, both historical and imaginative. Among them, George Goodwin's *Fatal Rivalry* gives a very readable account of the battle and the events leading up to it. Rosemary Goring's *Before Flodden* is a fictional account of Flodden's impact on a local family and Noel Hodgson's *Heron's Flight* gives a more involved drama-documentary account of the battle.

Background by **Andrew Ayre**

The Prisoner of War

The Prisoner of War **retold**

Not all the Tales are set in the Borders; some tell of Scots' adventures abroad. The Prisoner of War is a sequel to an earlier Tale, The Man-of-Wars Man, recounting the further travails of an Edinburgh man named Elder – first as a pressed man in the British Navy and then as a prisoner in France during the Napoleonic Wars.

Elder had gone to sea against his parents' wishes as an 'entered seaman' on a ship called the Latona. He had been at sea only a short time when he was swept overboard, and would have perished had he not been picked up by a merchantman bound for Scottish waters.

This Tale begins with his rescue. As he regains his youthful health and vigour on board, he becomes friendly with the mate, Mr Ross – who gives the naive Elder valuable information on the practice of impressment.

Elder remarked that when any vessel came in sight, "The men look as if they wished themselves anywhere but where they are". Ross explained that the sailors would be happy to engage with any French ship that they came upon, but the possibility of being deprived of their liberty by 'our own men-of-war' was an abiding fear.

To avoid the risk of impressment in the Firth of Forth they sailed further north to the Moray Firth, hoping to put ashore at Cromarty. But as they lay off the Sutors of Cromarty, their worst fears were realised: a British frigate appeared, with a manned boat making towards them.

Under orders from Ross they made a run for it; but their efforts were in vain. Along with his shipmates, Elder found himself on the Edgar, making sail for the Firth of Forth after all.

Firm naval discipline was exercised as they came in sight of Edinburgh. Elder had hoped to obtain leave, as had many of the other men who were natives of the city. But all requests were refused. He was able to send a letter to his father and to meet with him the following day. Although the meeting was not totally harmonious,

Elder's father undertook to try what he could to obtain his son's discharge.

Elder was touched by the plight of his mess mate, Wallace, a volunteer who had served in many sea encounters and had not been home for 10 years. Wallace had been promised two days' leave, and had 10 gold guineas saved for a celebration with friends and family. When orders came for the ship to leave immediately, he threw the money overboard in bitterness and disappointment – declaring that he might die in the ship's first action.

They sailed for the Nore, the Royal Naval anchorage in the Thames estuary which had been the scene of a riotous mutiny in May 1797.

At the Nore, Elder was drafted aboard the 64-gun Repulse. They sailed to patrol the coast of Brittany, keeping particular watch over Brest harbour, in constant search for French ships.

The Repulse.

Nelson had defeated the French at Aboukir Bay in 1799. This Battle of the Nile established British naval superiority for the rest of the Wars. But Napoleon kept his surviving squadrons ready for sea, thus keeping the Royal Navy at full stretch on blockade duties. Brest was one of France's three major naval bases; hence the need for vessels like the Repulse to block or hunt down any small French breakout force. Elder found these duties monotonous.

But the situation changed suddenly when they ran onto rocks one night in a storm. Despite the heavy seas rolling over them, Elder noted that discipline was maintained: "Everything had been done that skill and resolution could accomplish to save the vessel, but in vain". Dawn revealed a scene of imminent death, with a huge sea breaking over dangerous rocks as French peasants watched at the water's edge.

Detail from an original illustration to Wilson's Tales of the Borders.

James Paterson, a lad from Edinburgh, swam to shore with a line and despite enormous personal danger managed to reach land. A hawser was made fast to the line and secured on shore. There was now a clear possibility of survival. However, as the officers and crew reached shore they met with peasants who were intent on taking what they could from these English sailors who had been blockading their land and causing poverty, distress and misery. Many had firearms, and set about robbing the sailors of clothing and the few possessions they had managed to save as they were wrecked. One sailor resisted when his watch chain was seized: he was struck to the ground and killed with a blow from a musket.

The sailors and officers were guarded, shivering on the beach, while the peasants took all that drifted ashore. As night drew on they were marched into a "small, poverty-stricken-like town, with an old ruinous church and churchyard, surrounded by high walls, with an iron gate close by". Into this chill, desolate place they were herded, with gates locked and sentinels posted. They were fed, but only with black bread and water.

The religious beliefs of the time made the choice of a churchyard as a pen really frightening. Conditions were cramped and, as Elder noted, "By far the greater number of us believed as firmly in the reality of ghosts as we did in our own existence. Fear is contagious. We huddled together, and peered fearfully around, expecting every moment to see some appalling vision or hear some dreadful sound."

This was the setting in which the men started to tell ghost stories, whispering further horror into the already horrendous night. When Dick Bates sang the ballad *Hazier's Ghost*, they were thoroughly frightened by its spine-chilling evocation of the fate of Hosier and his sailors – who had also been on blockade duties, in the West Indies, over half a century before.

Another spine-chilling tale was told by Bob Nelson, the only one of the crew who claimed first-hand experience of ghosts. Nelson's tale concerned a family who were leaving Scotland for a new life in America. On the pier at Greenock, he had watched the family embarking, leaving on shore the wife's old mother. The mother cursed her son-in-law for taking her daughter away and vowed that "Dead or alive, I shall yet see my Mary". During the crossing the weather turned stormy and the little family was confined to their cabin; but while doing duty as steersman, Nelson was often aware of a presence he could not explain.

The weather settled as they neared New York and the children of the family came to play on deck. The mother was still very ill in her berth below. Then, suddenly, Nelson saw the old mother as he had last seen her at Greenock, on deck with her daughter, close to the children. As he watched, both women disappeared over the side of the ship. At that moment the captain came on deck with the news that the children's mother had just died. The story made Elder and his shipmates huddle together for protection from real and supernatural chill.

After this dreadful night the sailors regained their fighting spirit and played leapfrog to warm themselves up. Some climbed to the top of the walls of the confined space and shouted jeers and taunts at their French guards. Spontaneously, they burst into *God save the King*, followed by a rousing rendition of *Rule Britannia*, forgetting in their enthusiasm that they were prisoners, hungry, cold and naked.

Soon afterwards, two companies of soldiers arrived and a long, gruelling march began. The sailors and their captors fed themselves by trapping livestock from the already miserably poor villages they passed.

When they reached Rennes, Elder was moved by the kindness shown to them by a 'beautiful young lady' who supplied them with shoes for feet that had been cut and bruised by the condition of the roads. In the places they passed there were only old men, women and children, with women doing the work of men. Eventually they arrived at a prison, where they were allowed to go out and do the work of the men serving in Napoleon's forces.

Elder was employed as a cart and plough wright and reported into prison once a week. His employer was a closet Royalist: Citizen Vauquin was convinced that the glory of France lay in the courts of her kings. During the four months he remained a prisoner, Elder had several debates with Vauquin on liberty, free speech and 'equality being the law of the land': issues debated by many in those stormy revolutionary times. Vauquin told Elder of the violence and bloodshed which broke out after the execution of the king. He cited his own personal experiences with the lord of the chateau where he worked. Although the old lord had been despotic the young one, who befriended Vauquin, was enlightened; but, he said, to be rich and nobly born was now a crime of the deepest dye.

News came to Vauquin that the chateau was to be seized by the state. Fearing for his young master's life, he disguised the nobleman as one of his workmen and watched in horror as destruction followed. His concealment of the young lord was discovered and Vauquin was in danger of summary execution until, feigning loyalty to the Republican cause, he suggested that the chateau be set ablaze. The lord was imprisoned and would have lost his head; but Vauquin was able to effect a rescue, helping the lord to escape disguised as a peasant girl.

Vauquin remained at heart an ardent Royalist, giving only lip service to the Republican cause. He helped Elder in many ways, instructing him in French and drawing as well as encouraging him in a love of the arts.

After four months of this semi-imprisonment the sailors were marched to St-Malo on the coast, where an arrangement for an exchange of prisoners awaited them. Once more at sea, they were no sooner off Jersey than they were brought-to by the Ramilles. Crowded on board her, they were yet again impressed into service. This was the Navy's invidious practice at the time: to intercept and pressgang straight from the cartels that were used for the exchange of prisoners of war. Elder remained on the Ramilles until she was paid-off at the peace.

Retold by CF

Background to *The Prisoner of War*

The song referred to as *Hazier's Ghost* in the story was a 1740 ballad by Richard Glover, *Admiral Hosier's Ghost*. It was sung to a tune by Handel, *Come, listen to my ditty*.

The song recalls the Blockade of Porto Bello in the West Indies. In March 1726, Francis Hosier had been sent to command a squadron in Panama to prevent Spain from sending treasure home. He had 20 ships and could easily have captured the town, but he was under strict government orders which forbade him from firing a shot. He was therefore forced to cruise off the mosquito-infested coasts for several months. Yellow fever broke out, killing Hosier and between 3,000 and 4,000 of his men.

"This brave man, seeing his best officers and men daily swept away, his ships exposed to inevitable destruction, and himself made the sport of the enemy, is said to have died of a broken heart", wrote the 18th century Scottish author Tobias Smollett

In the 1730s the Government appeasement policies of men like Walpole, and not Hosier personally, were blamed for the disaster. Twelve years after Hosier's death, at the start of the War of Jenkin's Ear, Admiral Vernon captured Porto Bello with only six ships.

Admiral Vernon was a colourful character who created the 'recipe' which helped protect his sailors against scurvy. By diluting the rum ration with water and lime or lemon juice he effectively controlled excessive drunkenness and introduced vitamin C into his men's diet. His taking of Porto Bello was seen by the pro-war 'Patriots' opposed to Walpole as a just vengeance for Hosier's earlier enforced inaction. As a result of his victory he gained the freedom of the City of London and areas of London, Edinburgh and Dublin were named Portobello as a reminder of his triumph.

In the ballad, Glover describes Vernon's triumph being interrupted by Hosier's ghost. Hosier charges Vernon to draw attention to the forgotten affair in England so that the ghosts can find rest. Glover may well have written the poem as an attack on Walpole's half-hearted commitment to the war.

The poem deals with lost honour and regret. Had Hosier obeyed his instincts rather than orders, he would not have sacrificed his personal integrity. He might well have been branded a traitor but he would yet have 'played an English part'. So, in the midst of Vernon's triumph, Hosier's fate and that of his captains and sailors serve as a potent reminder that sometimes obeying orders can lead to death and loss of reputation.

As a ghost story it forms part of the highly charged, supernatural atmosphere Wilson created in this section of *The Prisoner of War*. These are the words Dick Bates sang:

As, near Porto Bello lying,
On the gently swelling flood,
At midnight, with streamers flying,
Our triumphant navy rode;
There, while Vernon sate, all glorious
From the Spaniards' late defeat,
And his crew, with shouts victorious,
Drank success to England's fleet,
On a sudden, shrilly sounding,
Hideous yells and shrieks were heard;
Then, each heart with fears confounding,
A sad troop of ghosts appear'd;
All in dreary hammocks shrouded,
Which for winding sheets they wore;
And with looks by sorrow clouded,
Frowning on that hostile shore.
On them gleam'd the moon's wan lustre,
When the shade of Hosier brave,
His pale band was seen to muster,
Rising from their wat'ry grave;
O'er the glimmering wave he hied him,

Where the Burford rear'd her sail,
With 3,000 ghosts beside him,
And in groans did Vernon hail.
"Heed, oh heed! My fatal story,
I am Hosier's injur'd ghost;
You who now have purchas'd glory
At this place where I was lost;
Tho' in Porto Bello's ruin
You now triumph, free from fears,
Yet to hear of my undoing,
You will mix your joys with tears.
See yon mournful spectres sweeping,
Ghastly, o'er this hated wave,
Whose wan cheeks are stain'd with weeping;
These were English captains brave;
And these numbers pale and horrid,
Were my sailors once so bold;
Lo, each hangs his drooping forehead,
While his dismal tale is told.
I, by 20 sail attended,
Did this Spanish town affright,
Nothing then its wealth defended

But my orders not to fight;
Oh that, with my wrath complying,
I had cast them in the main,
Then, no more inactive lying,
I had low'red the pride of Spain.
For resistance I could fear none,
But with 20 ships had done,
What thou, brave and happy Vernon,
Did'st achieve with six alone.
Then the Bastimentos never
Had our foul dishonour seen,
Nor the sea the sad receiver
Of these gallant men had been.
Thus, like thee, proud Spain dismaying,
And her galleons leading home,
Tho' condemn'd for disobeying,
I had met a traitor's doom;
To have fall'n, my country crying,
'He has played an English part',
Has been better far than dying
Of a griev'd and broken heart.

Unrepining at thy glory,
Thy successful arms we hail,
But remember our sad story,
When to Britain back you sail!,
All your country's foes subduing,
When your patriot friends you see,
Think on vengeance for my ruin,
And for England sham'd in me."

Background by CF

The Monomaniac

The Surgeon's Tale: The Monomaniac **dramatised**

This is one of the later Tales, part of a series entitled Sketches from a Surgeon's Note-book. These may have been written by Alexander Allan Carr, a surgeon who practised a few miles from Berwick, in Coldingham and Ayton. This dramatisation of the story was written by another Borders doctor, Dr Michael A Fenty.

A darkened bedroom. ISABELLA Cunninghame sits in a chair, staring through the audience into the distance.

Isabella's MOTHER enters with a DOCTOR, carrying an oil lamp. Isabella turns her head away from them.

DOCTOR   So this is the patient, your daughter? And her condition? Her symptoms?

MOTHER   She sits daily in a darkened room... she cannot stand the light. She has been like this for 18 months... ever since she returned from India.

DOCTOR   From India... interesting. What took her so far from home?

MOTHER   Love... and marriage to the man she loved – George Cunninghame.

49

(Moving behind ISABELLA, picks up portrait from the bedside table)

> They were childhood sweethearts. Neither of them even looked at another – not even when they were parted, while he made his way in the world. For five years he was away – first in London, then in India. He was always destined for a mariner's life, like his father before him.
>
> When he returned, they were wed. And scarcely two months later, thanks to his earlier endeavours, he was given command of an Indiaman, The Griffin, sailing to Madras. Isabella went with him.
>
> You have no idea the experience she has suffered… it is a miracle that her mind survived it.

DOCTOR *(Talking over ISABELLA'S head to MOTHER)* Her mind, you say… so this is not just some affliction of the eyes that troubles the young lady?

MOTHER She may tell you the whole story herself… all I will say is that she has had what I would call a fit… a faint… brought on by a hallucination: a vision of her dear dead husband, who died on that voyage and who she saw committed to the depths of the Indian Ocean. This vision has recurred again and again.

> But ask her yourself… hear her story.

DOCTOR *(Confiding, to MOTHER)* It sounds as if she is in the grip of a rare condition that we call… monomania…

(MOTHER appears perplexed)

> …idée fixe… a single or solitary delusion.

MOTHER Ah, yes. Indeed it is so… But please… ask her yourself. Hear her story.

DOCTOR steps forward and coughs politely to gain ISABELLA'S attention. She turns.

DOCTOR   Mrs Cunninghame, please excuse me.

ISABELLA resumes staring at the wall

I am the local doctor and – though no specialist – your mother, in her concern for you has asked me to examine your eyes and see if there is a cause for your photophobia... your aversion to light.

ISABELLA nods

DOCTOR   ...and your mother also mentioned the matter of these... visions... which have so troubled you. Perhaps you may wish to discuss them?

ISABELLA continues staring at the wall

DOCTOR   Well, first... please... may I examine your eyes?

She faces him, with a blank expression. As he talks, he moves a finger in front of her face. Her eyes follow it.

DOCTOR   I can see no obvious cause for your aversion to light...

But please, tell me of your voyage to India. What occurred may have caused your symptoms... and, er, those your mother mentioned...

She said you had been subject to fainting... and fearful ... ahem... hallucinations?

ISABELLA   *(Sharply)* I am not mad.

DOCTOR   Oh – of that I am assured! But ... please... tell me what happened on that trip ... it may be helpful

ISABELLA   At first, I was naturally apprehensive of such a voyage... all the way to India! But I had such love for my George and such faith in him! And I quickly came to enjoy the life on a great three-masted sailing ship.

She turns to face the audience

There was another lady on board – a Mrs Hardy, bound for Cape Town with two servant girls. The First Officer was called Crawley and the Second Mate was a man named Buist. The rest of the crew, I saw little of – life is hard on a sailing ship and the men were busy.

There was a steward – a German called Kreutz. I did not like the look of him – and George, when I mentioned it, did say he wasn't too sure of him. But he'd had no choice in picking the crew.

At the Cape, Mrs Hardy disembarked and her two servants went ashore. One had agreed to stay with me to Madras – but did not come back aboard.

I went to George to delay sailing, but Crawley pointed out that a favourable wind had sprung up... so we departed under a stiff gale for Mozambique.

SAILOR 1 *(off)* Hoist the mainsail! Do you want to miss this wind?

SAILOR 2 *(off)* Aye aye!

ISABELLA We were following the coast of Madagascar. George told me stories of the cannibalism that had been reported there. I suppose he meant to distract me. But all it did was frighten me and make me even more anxious.

Especially when the wind dropped and we were becalmed off that fearful place.

At night I couldn't sleep.

I would walk the deck, seeing the fires of the natives on the shore and imagining all sorts of horrors. The air was still, the sea was like glass, and the sails hung loose on the masts.

The men were listless... and all the time that dark forbidding coastline filled my gaze.

DOCTOR *(Quiet, musing)* Yes... It would seem that you were already in a state of nervous exhaustion... the lack of sleep... the lack of female company... the lurid tales on an overwrought mind... yes, yes...

ISABELLA But worse, far worse, was to come.

GEORGE enters, lies on bed in a beam of steel-blue light

ISABELLA As I wandered the deck, Kreutz came to me. He said the captain – my George – was ill!

(Runs to bed) I rushed to the cuddy cabin he used and found my beloved George in agony with spasms of pain in his stomach and chest. He lay there vomiting.

GEORGE Oh, God Isabella – what's happening to me? I'm dying... That villain Cr... *(He passes out)*

ISABELLA I did not know whose name he was trying to say. Crawley? Kreutz? But at that moment, he passed out.

The second mate, Buist, came in. I asked him what he thought had happened to George but he just looked wildly and shook his head.

I nursed George but he was obviously dying. I could hear the voices of the men, Crawley, Kreutz and Buist and the tread of their feet on the deck above.

George raved wildly...

GEORGE *(Quietly in the background as Isabella speaks over him)* Isabella... see the bird there? Come on, run! Get the mainsail up... stow that gear... oh my love... oh Isabella... You there, bring her round to port!...

What's this? Kreutz? Crawley?

53

ISABELLA *(speaking over George)* ...unconnected words, some about our childhood, some about the ship and his command, some about the crew, his distrust of Kreutz – all deranged and mixed up.

(When GEORGE finishes raving)

Then he turned, staring at me... reached out... and I saw the life leave him.

The light on GEORGE goes out

I screamed and rushed out on to the deck. *(Moves urgently forward)* I fear I might have thrown myself overboard but Crawley seized me and dragged me back. *(Throws herself backwards into chair)*

GEORGE vanishes quietly

ISABELLA He and Kreutz came to the cuddy. They undressed George and wound a large sheet around his body. As they worked, I could not bear to look at the lamp and after they left I dimmed its flame and sat with my dear George in near-darkness. Lying there in the long white shroud...

I pulled back the folds and kissed his dear face... I must have slept...

DOCTOR *(Behind her)* You were exhausted, my dear. The sleep was a reflex – a protective reflex from the brain.

ISABELLA When I came to, I heard voices again: Crawley and Kreutz

CRAWLEY and KREUTZ step forward to the bedposts, leaning on them as rigging. Their faces are underlit, as if by moonlight reflected from the sea.

CRAWLEY When the wind starts, it will be from the North. We should make all speed for Rio...

KREUTZ   Ja, then get rid of the cargo and head for the West Indies.

CRAWLEY   Right, Hans, get the carpenter to knock up a coffin – we'll put the body over the side tomorrow.

KREUTZ   But what do we do with her?

CRAWLEY   Put her ashore – the natives will find a use for her.

KREUTZ   We're still becalmed, don't forget. There's no wind to carry us out of this channel…

CRAWLEY   None to bring no one looking for us neither. Come on – the body… let's get it up on deck.

Moonlight off, CRAWLEY and KREUTZ vanish.

ISABELLA They came and ordered me back to my cabin. Before they could take him, I pulled back the sheet and kissed my beloved George for the last time. His pale face was imprinted on my eyes and mind.

          I could not bring myself to go on deck even to see my dear husband being committed to the sea.

CRAWLEY and KREUTZ reappear in the moonlight.

KREUTZ   *(Looking down into the water)* Mein Gott! The coffin is split open in the water!

CRAWLEY   The body's just floating down there. Oh God… we need a wind to get us out of here!

Moonlight off, CRAWLEY and KREUTZ vanish.

ISABELLA I lay in my cabin for days, in the dark.

          Kreutz brought me food but I could not eat. The ship was still becalmed. I expected at any time to be put ashore…

          (Hysterical) I was terrified for my life!

MOTHER *(Quietly)* There is more.

Crawley tried to force his attentions on her.

(DOCTOR is aghast) He killed her husband, then he came to her and suggested... it's unthinkable! He said... she could still be 'the wife of a ship's captain'.

(Agitated) Oh, that my poor girl should have to suffer such a loathsome man. He said if she did not consent to him he would put her ashore. She could become the wife of some native in... Madagascar!

DOCTOR *(Musing)* Even more stress for your mind to cope with. It is little wonder you are haunted by these memories.

ISABELLA *(Quietly)* I did think of killing myself. Or killing Crawley...

I had hidden a knife... but I couldn't kill anyone – not him, not myself.

I defied him for several days.

MOTHER That she should have been in such a position ... my poor daughter trapped by such a monster!

ISABELLA *(Rising to her feet and moving to the audience. Quiet, spooky.)* At night I went up on deck, I gazed on the dark waters where my George had been put. I was in despair.

Then I saw him... my husband... still in the white sheet... torn open to reveal his face... floating in the black waters – floating upright! – lit only by the moon...

His face, blue-white, with his eyes staring at me... Even with my love for him, I was shocked... I could not move. Those eyes held me. I heard Crawley and Kreutz coming, so I tore myself away and hid.

CRAWLEY and KREUTZ reappear in the moonlight.

CRAWLEY *(Whispers)* It's there... like his ghost is... is holding us here. And still no wind to get us out of here.

KREUTZ Damn that carpenter! The weights must have slipped to the feet when the coffin split...

CRAWLEY Those eyes staring at the ship... I can't stand it... Here, Kreutz: offer 20 guineas to any man that will sink that body.

KREUTZ But the men don't like it. They are superstitious... I think they may turn against us.

They exchange an anxious look. Moonlight off, CRAWLEY and KREUTZ vanish.

ISABELLA I heard the men coming and I rushed back to my cabin, not knowing what the outcome would be.

SAILOR 1 *(off)* It's a curse on the ship... The captain wants revenge – he'll hold us here 'til he gets it.

SAILOR 2 *(off)* It's them as killed him! He wants justice... get them or he'll never let us go!

ISABELLA I heard fighting on the deck. What was to be my fate now?

(She sits) And then they came to my cabin. It was Buist, who had retaken the ship. He said Crawley and Kreutz were dead, and George was revenged. I looked out of the cabin window and saw the corpse still watching the ship with those dead eyes... in the moonlight.

I implored Buist to recover his body and rebury him with proper dignity and that they did next day... along with the bodies of Crawley and Kreutz.

(DOCTOR and MOTHER exchange glances of revulsion)

The very next day a wind sprang up and the ship sailed as if released from a spell. We made good time to India. I remained there for two months…

But I found it hard to put into words my experiences and the sights I had seen… the pale face of my George and his unblinking eyes watching from the sea…

(Pause) I see them still.

DOCTOR *(to Mother)* Yes, this would seem to be a true case of monomania… brought on by the stresses and fears of events on the Indiaman and grief at the loss of her beloved husband. The fixed vision of his corpse floating by the ship… staring… is imprinted on her retinae and brain… An idée fixe…

(Gesturing to MOTHER to move to the door)

Such a condition is difficult to treat. I will continue to visit… perhaps some catharsis will occur… some final act.

DOCTOR and MOTHER reach the door and prepare to leave.

ISABELLA remains in her chair. She is seeing her beloved GEORGE, beckoning her from afar. She raises her hands as if trying to reach him…

Suddenly she throws herself forward, holding out her arms…

ISABELLA *(Screams)* George! George!

ISABELLA collapses on the floor. DOCTOR and MOTHER rush to her.

DOCTOR takes her pulse and shakes his head.

MOTHER *(Turns to audience)* It would seem the spectre of George Cunninghame had finally claimed his true love… from the depths of the Indian Ocean, he summoned her…

Strange things happen at sea.

Dramatised by **Dr Michael A Fenty**

Background to *The Monomaniac*

First published over 150 years ago, this Tale is a very early attempt to describe what we would now call post-traumatic stress disorder. What the doctor described as 'hallucinations' we'd now call 'persistent re-experiencing of the traumatic events' – or flashbacks.

When this Tale was written, the idea of 'monomania' was quite new. It was first described by a French psychiatrist around 1810. So maybe the person who wrote this Tale had some specialist knowledge. After all, this is one of several stories that were published as *The Surgeon's Tales*.

After Wilson died, other contributors were brought in to meet the public's demand for more Wilson's Tales. And we know that one of them was Alexander Allan Carr, a surgeon who practised in Coldingham and Ayton. Did he write *The Monomaniac*? Whoever it was, it certainly looks as if he'd observed post-traumatic stress at first hand.

And judging by the other Surgeon's Tales, he also knew quite a bit about bereavement, sleepwalking and suicide… But that's another Tale!

Dr Fenty's dramatisation was first performed for an evening of Wilson's Tales retellings in Paxton House, just over the border from Berwick, in October 2014. A film version was shot on location in Paxton House in April 2015.

The cast was:
Isabella: Abi Hood
Doctor & Crawley: Joe Lang
Mother: Jackie Kaines Lang
George & Kreutz: Stuart Faed

Background by **Joe Lang**

Launcelot Errington and his Nephew Mark:
A Tale of Lindisferne

Launcelot Errington **retold**

A favourite Tale of how two plucky adventurers captured Lindisfarne Castle "with moonlight and salmon fin" during the 1715 Jacobite Rising.

Everyone in Islandshire knows the adventures of Lancelot Errington, skipper of a coasting brig, and Mark, his favourite nephew and mate, and how they sailed into the Holy Island roads in October 1715. They were regular and welcome visitors, often bringing 'real genuine moonlight' – brandy or jenever from Holland. But on this occasion the islanders were puzzled, for there was no moonlight, the brig looked in good nick, and the weather was fair.

Lancelot considered himself a 'seasoned cask', well able to take his drink, and soon both he and Mark had taken enough of 'the creature' to have both eyes well watered. Mark assured his uncle that he was a true Errington and loyal to the King, James, and not to George, and that any secret plans would be safe with him. Lancelot took him into his confidence, explaining how he had met an important Northumbrian Jacobite, Thomas Foster, part of the family that owned Bamburgh Castle. Thomas had been High Sheriff of Northumberland in 1703, Member of Parliament for 1705 to 1708, and was now General of Jacobite forces south of the Tweed. Together they had a plan to seize Lindisfarne castle.

Mark, understandably, was sceptical. He pointed out that a single cannon shot from the battery would sink the brig. Lancelot, well oiled with moonlight, accused his nephew of being as thick as the upper works of a millstone, before explaining his cunning plan. This involved plenty of brandy and a couple of salmon.

One of the crew was hastily dispatched to Goswick across the Low, the safe route over the sands, to fetch the said fish. While awaiting his return, Lancelot calmly explained the principles of undermining a castle with a salmon fin. Then, leaving Mark in command, he set off for the castle, pipe in hand.

As luck would have it, he met the sergeant in command heading down the narrow path towards the village. Lancelot immediately enquired regarding news of King George, thus putting himself on the right side of the sergeant. He was told that the troublesome Pretender was back in Scotland and, worse, was heading south. Lancelot, gaining his confidence, invited his new acquaintance back to his brig for a tipple... and some fresh salmon. Chadwell, for that was the sergeant's name, took little persuading. Soon enough he, Lancelot and Mark were sat around the captain's table. Further mellowed with moonlight, Chadwell soon agreed that most of his men should join them. And so they did, in double quick order, leaving only a sentinel on guard at the castle gate, with two corporals and a gunner.

The moonlight flowed freely, and the good company ate and drank with relish. One glass followed another, and another. And yet another, until they ran out of fingers and lost count. Meanwhile, the tide rose, the wind whipped up the spume, and great waves crashed on the rocks at the harbour entrance. The brig began to rock and roll like a drunkard, and the unfamiliar movement, together with the strong spirit, quickly rendered Chadwell and his company both supine and insensible.

Lancelot gestured to Mark to follow him on deck. There he instructed boatswain Bob to keep a weather eye on the soldiers below and prevent them venturing ashore, using his handspike if need be. Soon uncle and nephew were at the castle gates, a sentinel before them. While Lancelot offered him a welcome swig from his hipflask, Mark deftly floored him as he tipped his head, tying him hand and foot, and picking up his musket.

The pair then ventured into the very heart of the castle, surprising a sleepy corporal, who was quickly disarmed and neatly trussed. The third soldier, sensing something amiss, descended the narrow stairs from the battery, musket raised and ready to fire. Lancelot beat him to it, winging him with leadshot in his shoulder. The shot roused the old gunner, a tough looking nut indeed, tight lipped and determined. Dragging the others to a locked room, Lancelot commanded the gunner to unlock the armoury. He refused, despite threats to suspend him down the sheer north face of the castle, then drop him to the rocks below for the seagulls' breakfast.

Tossing about in the air, grim reaper in the offing, the gunner's courage failed him, and so he relented. They hauled him back up and secured him under lock and key with his fellow soldiers. In no time every musket and cannon in the castle was loaded, primed, and ready to fire. Next the Union Flag was ripped down and the Royal Standard of the House of Stuart raised in its place. Standing before the castle gate, fishermen and villagers marvelled at the doings of bold skipper Errington and his nephew Mark, secretly admiring their courage and ingenuity.

Then two mighty cannon blasts rent the air and set a hundred seagulls flapping and mewing into the sky above the harbour. The villagers beat a hasty retreat. Lancelot, having raided the castle's cellar as well as its armoury, cracked open a fine bottle of port. "I hereby proclaim our only lawful sovereign James, the Third of England and Ninth of Scotland, king of these realms. God save the King! May all traitors be choked." Thus they drank their chosen king's health.

But Mark was restive, pacing and re-pacing the length of the long gallery, looking longingly towards Bamburgh. Lancelot was quick to spot the lovelorn countenance in his nephew's eyes: Mark was pining for his Sally. More pressing still, he was wondering how the two of them could possibly hold the castle against the garrison at Berwick, who would surely be heading their way sooner or later. Easy to take with moonlight and salmon fin, but not so easy to hold, eh, uncle ?

Lancelot was quick to reassure, explaining that General Foster's men would surely, even as he spoke, be assembling behind Beal Bushes ready to cross the Low; and that there were two French privateers lying snugly enough behind the Farne Islands, just waiting for the signal from the cannon before setting sail for Lindisferne. Little did Lancelot know that the French privateers had run into a strong northerly gale as they beat their way up the channel, and were now sheltering off the Dutch coast; nor that Foster's men had been flushed from the Kyloe Hills by reinforcements loyal to King George, en route to the Scottish border. Nor that the commander of the garrison at Berwick, hearing the cannon signal, had taken up his telescope and spied the Royal Standard of the House of Stuart fluttering merrily in the breeze above the castle. The effrontery of it!

Three companies of infantry, and artillery, were soon to be seen leaving Berwick and hastening across Tweedmouth Moor to Beal Bushes. There they waited for the ebb before making safe passage over the Low to the island.

Nor did Mark know that Sally, too, had heard the cannon. Guessing what might be happening, she had hastened to Belford for extra provisions. Or that Thomas Foster, from his vantage point high up on the battlements of Bamburgh Castle, looked thoughtful, then resolute, and ordered his best man to ride hotfoot to Alnmouth with a message for a certain Captain Boulmer, well known to him and Lancelot.

Meantime, back on the brig, Sergeant Chadwell and his men, nursing sore heads, had stumbled on deck. They attracted the attention of the crews of several boats that had been out herring fishing, who, pulling alongside the brig, quickly separated Boatswain Bob from his handspike, and helped the soldiers ashore. The sergeant and his company hot-footed it to the castle gates, in as orderly a fashion as possible, given their drunken disposition. There they found Mark, keeping guard from the battlement above. Chadwell's remonstrations, and the sundry stones and rocks hurled at Mark, were in vain. In fact Mark retaliated by levelling his firelock and raking the sergeant's right cheek, carrying away part of his ear. The soldiers soon fled in search of safety and succour, a sorry sight indeed, with Mark's laughter ringing in their ears.

It was not long before the soldiers from Berwick had traversed the Low and set up their artillery at the castle gates. Meantime their commander, having first arrested Chadwell and his men for gross dereliction of duty, had them locked in St Mary's Church. Next he made himself known to Lancelot, demanding that he surrender. Lancelot was defiant, claiming that there was no such word as surrender in any dictionary in the castle, and that he therefore didn't know what he meant.

There followed the most spirited defence by these two brave kinsmen, a long and desperate resistance. Finally, the gates breached, they were forced to retreat down the very cliff from which they had dangled the hapless gunner. Running for the beach, seeing the tide in, they plunged in and struck out for the mainland. To no avail. A dozen soldiers caught up with them, muskets ready. Ever defiant, Lancelot reminded Mark that "They who are born to be drowned will never be hanged", and to fear nothing. Carted unceremoniously to Berwick, they were incarcerated in the Marygate gaol, together with sundry debtors and felons, to await trial and certain doom. Meanwhile, they created a wondrous sensation in the town.

Even more wondrous, they remained in high spirits – singing like larks and, being good Catholics, refusing the offerings of the prison chaplain. As on Holy Island, and indeed across Islandshire, there were many sympathetic to the Jacobite cause. News of her swain soon reached Sally Beadnell. Prisoners often suspended a can from their windows, with a petition to well-wishers to "Remember the poor prisoners". Sally brought an unusually heavy loaf of bread. On breaking into it, Mark was astonished to find a chisel. Some days later, the gaoler found all the cells empty. In Lancelot's cell a great flagstone had been lifted and a tunnel ran down and out into Marygate.

The alarum raised, constables ran hither and thither in pursuit of the escapees. Not quickly enough. Under cover of darkness Lancelot and Mark hot-footed it down Hide Hill, through Shore Gate, and onto the pier. Spying the Customs House boat, they rowed for their lives across the Tweed to Carr Rock at Spittal. They headed for one of Lancelot's fisher friends, where, welcomed, victualled and watered, they were stowed out of sight.

For 10 days they remained in the stow-hole. Meantime, the hue and cry intensified, with a reward of £500 on their heads, a king's ransom in those days. Lancelot was not without enemies, and one got wind of their hidey-hole. So it was that, had you been up on Scremerston Moor, you would have spied two comely fishwives, decked in yellow headscarves, long skirts, creels slung over shoulders, but with curiously deep voices, moving urgently south to Bamburgh. On reaching the Kyloes, they rested up until dark, with a clear view of Holy Island. Much to Mark's consternation, his uncle's brig had disappeared. Lancelot was quick to reassure his nephew regarding any inheritance that might eventually come his way. Elector George's sharks could do what they liked with his brig he said, referring mysteriously to something more handsome that they could not touch.

Around midnight the two kinsmen set out towards Bamburgh and Sally Beadnell's farm. At about three in the morning young Sally was awoken by a gentle tapping at her bedroom window. Half expecting to see her handsome young Mark, she was quite taken aback to be confronted by two uncouth looking Spittal fishwives! Quickly reassured that it really was her lover and his uncle, she bustled them into the house and, over a brew of tea, she warned them that the whole county was on the lookout for them. It was known that she was friendly with Mark, indeed already suspected of harbouring the fugitives, so no one could be trusted, not even her father's labourers. Worst of all, Foster's rebel army had been defeated, and he was now locked up in Newgate Gaol.

It was an agonising scene in that farmhouse kitchen as dawn broke over the Farnes. The two kinsmen prepared to die rather than surrender, assuring young Sally that they would all meet in heaven.

Lovesick, tearful and distraught, she clung to Mark for dear life. But she quickly gathered herself, rallied, and told them of her plan. They were to hole up in a pea-stack out beyond the steading until the hue and cry subsided, confident that no one would think of looking there and that she could feed and water them each night. She brooked no concern for her danger: if they were destined to die, she would wish nothing better than to pass over to the next world in their good company. Meanwhile, she would tell no one, not even her own father, as any implicated in harbouring fugitives faced certain death.

"... she was quite taken aback to be confronted by two uncouth looking Spittal fishwives!"
An original illustration from Wilson's Tales of the Borders.

Nine days passed, and her secret held, even when two soldiers returned to search the farm, and poked and prodded the pea-stack, curious that the Erringtons were still at large, and eyeing the beautiful Sally with interest. On the tenth day came cold winds and stormclouds, and the stock were getting hungry. The thrashing man came into the farmhouse kitchen to seek Mr Beadnell's say-so to start thrashing the pea-stack.

Unfortunately, Sally's look of consternation was plain for all to see. The thrashing-man spotted her anxiety and quickly surmised the reason for it, remembering the £500 reward on the Erringtons' heads. His suspicions were heightened when Sally pleaded with her father to send his man to Alnwick first thing in the morning, on an urgent errand for her – they were running low on provisions. It was agreed, the man was dismissed, and Mr Beadnell sat his distraught daughter down by the range, and explained that he knew everything, that Lancelot was his good friend, and that he feared she had betrayed him, albeit unwittingly.

There was nothing for it but to pack the fugitives off post haste, not a moment to lose. The good father and his daughter prepared provisions, money and stout country garb, and then explained all to the kinsmen. Soon after midnight, they were again on the road, heading south towards Alnmouth. Not long after leaving, and hearing a body of men heading for the farm, they prayed for the Beadnells' safety. The pea-stack was razed to the ground, but, finding nothing, they moved on. As for the treacherous thrashing-man, Mr Beadnell threw him out of the house. Ever honest, he threw his wages after him.

After spending the day holed-up in a hedge inland from Craster, our defiant Jacobites set out for Alnmouth under cover of darkness. Early next morning, Captain Boulmer, standing on the foredeck of his brig, was not entirely surprised – but certainly very much relieved – to see two very agricultural characters coming down the jetty towards him. The tide being high, they set sail down the Aln and crossed over the bar within the hour, bound for safe haven – Dieppe on the Normandy coast, where both men were well known.

Not so long after their arrival there, young Mark received a letter from Sally, with some interesting news about his uncle's brig. A wealthy but rogueish gentleman neighbour, who had made it clear on occasion to Mr Beadnell that he wished to marry his beautiful daughter, had come by way of Lancelot's brig. Moreover, Sally had it on good authority that the brig had been seen in North Sunderland harbour, loading herring barrels, bound for Hamburg.

The kinsmen wasted no time leaving Dieppe. Two days later they were in Hamburg, in the guise of German merchants, sporting beards, moustaches, and, in very broken English, seeking passage to England. Soon they were well out in the channel, by which time the captain had re-acquainted himself with the bottle, his boon companion. Indeed he had already indulged 'potations pottle deep'. So it was but the work of a moment for Mark to take him unawares and tie him up in his cabin. Meanwhile Lancelot disabled the helmsman and, pointing his pistol at him, ordered the crew to be gathered. He confirmed that he was once again the rightful master of his brig, unlawfully wrested from him.

The helmsman, recognising his old skipper beneath the disguise, embraced him warmly – before, in low voice, warning him that the captain and his mate were not to be trusted. They were rapidly set adrift in the stern-boat with sufficient biscuits, beef, water and rum to see them ashore. Later that day the brig docked at Tilbury and offloaded her cargo. Lancelot then struck out for Newgate Gaol, where Thomas Foster was destined for the scaffold for treason against the King. No doubt moonlight played its part: the details remain shrouded in mystery, but by hook or by crook Lancelot rescued his old friend from an unwelcome rendezvous with the hangman. Shortly before dawn the brig could be seen well out in the Thames estuary, eastward bound for France and freedom.

As to the rest of my tale, in time King George issued a general pardon to all Jacobites. Our kinsmen returned to their beloved Northumberland. Mark took over as the skipper of the brig and married his Sally, who bore him many children. Lancelot lived on until, on hearing of Bonnie Prince Charlie's defeat at Culloden in 1746, full of grief and age, he shuffled off this mortal coil.

And so, dear reader, next time you look upon Holy Island, or visit Lindisferne Castle, remember the daring exploits of Lancelot Errington and his favourite young nephew Mark.

Retold by **Nick Jones**

Background to *Launcelot Errington*

Lindisfarne Castle and Harbour today. Photograph by Andrew Ayre.

Holy Island, off the coast of North Northumberland, has long been a cultural icon and, with Lindisfarne Castle, a popular feature on the tourism map. Its brief moment of glory in the 1715 Rising, when Lancelot and Mark Errington captured the castle for the Jacobites, is now virtually unknown, though for a while the two were famous for it. No wonder Wilson based a Tale on this remarkable event.

His narrative sweep and vivid portrayal of the protagonists, despite the somewhat clichéd 'nautical dialogue', are based on good local knowledge and historical fact. Wilson has clearly researched the period thoroughly – apart from one unfortunate slip when he has the Erringtons, after replacing the Union flag at the castle with the Royal Stuart standard as a signal to the expected French invasion force, proclaim their exiled sovereign 'James the Third of England and Ninth of Scotland' (instead of Eighth).

Wilson adapts or deletes historical material to serve his artistic purpose. For example, towards the Tale's end, he gives Lancelot the credit for rescuing General Thomas Forster from Newgate Gaol; whereas it was a heroine of the Rising, Dorothy Forster, Thomas's sister, who organised it. She travelled to London through ice and snow just days before his trial, riding pillion with an Adderstone blacksmith, Purdy, who made a cast of the key to the prison cell door. She then bribed the gaoler (probably with money from her uncle, Lord Crewe) and arranged for him to be locked up in her brother's place so that Thomas could escape to France.

Wilson chooses not to use some of the recorded details of how the Erringtons overpowered the master gunner at the castle, Samuel Philipson. The real Philipson's army pay was in arrears so he earned extra money by setting up as a barber; Lancelot called on him, asked for a shave and then left the castle, returning later with his nephew on the pretext of having lost his watch-key. Instead, Wilson bases his narrative on Lancelot's promise of brandy and salmon on board his ship to most of the garrison, and his feigned sympathy for the sentinel missing out on the entertainment. He also gives his own version of the struggle that ensued on the battery – omitting the throwing of a grenade by the gunner at Lancelot, who was luckily unharmed, and the screams of "Murder!" by Mrs Philipson, who makes no appearance in the story.

What lay behind the Erringtons' spectacular, if short-lived, achievement?

The term 'Jacobite' comes from 'Jacobus', Latin for James, and signifies a supporter of the exiled Stuart 'kings over the water'. This initially meant King James II of England and Ireland (James VII of Scotland), who was deposed in 1685 in a political coup, the so-called 'Glorious Revolution', by his nephew and son-in-law, Prince William of Orange (who became William III) and his own daughter, Princess Mary (who ruled jointly with her husband as Mary II).

William had landed with an army of 14,000 Dutchmen, to investigate (so he said) the birth of a son to James by his second wife, Mary Beatrice of Modena. James's two daughters by his first wife, Mary and Anne, were Protestant. The new male heir had displaced Princess Mary, who he had always hoped would bring him the Crown and English support in his struggle to prevent the

French from taking over the Netherlands. The transparent lie that the baby was really a commoner's son, smuggled into the palace in a warming-pan to replace a stillborn child, was put about because of the prospect of a line of Catholic kings after James died. It was refuted by the attendance of 42 witnesses at the birth.

Normally a brave man but faced with this crisis and deserted by his commanders, including John Churchill (soon to be created Duke of Marlborough by William), James had some sort of nervous breakdown and fled into exile in France. This allowed William to make his successful pitch for power.

After James II died in 1701, 'Jacobite' signified a supporter of his son, Prince James Francis Edward Stuart, recognised as James III of England and VIII of Scotland by France, Spain, the Papal States and Modena. This James was later called the Old Pretender (meaning claimant) by his Hanoverian enemies, who won the power struggle in Britain between different branches of the same royal family following James's forced 'abdication'.

Queen Anne, Mary's younger sister and successor to William, continued ruling after her husband's death. When she died, her place as ruler was taken not by her Catholic half-brother, James, the rightful king whom she had supplanted, but by her second cousin, Georg Ludwig, Elector of Hanover, crowned as George I in 1714. George was the next heir by the terms of the Act of Settlement (1701), which barred Catholics from the throne. Parliament had had to skip over 57 blood relatives of Anne with a better claim than George's mother (the Electress Sophia, James VI and I's granddaughter, who died less than two months before Anne did) to find a successor who was Protestant. Anne had had 17 children, including miscarriages and still-births, by her husband, Prince George of Denmark, but died childless. Her longest surviving child, Prince William, Duke of Gloucester, died at the age of 11. She was the last crowned monarch of the House of Stuart.

The 1715 Rising (the '15 for short), was one of several plots and risings in favour of a Stuart restoration over a period of more than 55 years from 1689 onwards. These were a very real danger to William III, George I and his son, George II. The '15 had a far better chance of succeeding than the later, better-known 1745 Rising (known as the '45). In 1715, the new Hanoverian dynasty had been established for only a year and was proving very unpopular, both in its policies and in the person of George I. George lacked charm and never bothered to learn English, being more interested in Hanover than Britain, so a restoration of the Stuart monarchy was a distinct possibility.

What the '15 lacked was a clear game-plan, effective communication with forces in other parts of Britain (difficult in that age), an experienced general and a charismatic leader. The outcome might well have been different if James FitzJames, 1st Duke of Berwick (illegitimate son of James II by Arabella Churchill), had not failed to commit himself to the Rising, even though James III was his half-brother as well as his king. Or if the figurehead and active participant had been Prince Charles Edward Stuart rather than his worthy but lacklustre father, James III. But in 1715 the Duke of Berwick excused himself from military command, and Prince Charles Edward had not even been born.

One problem for any Jacobite rising was that it had to be directed at a distance from the rival Jacobite royal court abroad. The first court in exile was based at the château of Saint-Germain, near Paris, given by Louis XIV to James II. When the latter's son, James III, became a political embarrassment to the French, he was forced to quit French territory by the terms of the 1713 Treaty of Utrecht between France and Great Britain. He settled first – and at the time of the '15 – at Bar-le-Duc in the independent Duchy of Lorraine. Subsequently, he moved his court to Avignon (a Papal enclave), Urbino and finally, in 1719, Rome. He awaited his restoration to his father's British thrones for over 65 years. And when he died at the age of 78, the Jacobite cause was carried on in his name by his son, Prince Charles Edward (the Young Pretender).

Although the exiled Stuart sovereigns were Catholic, neither the '15 nor the later '45 was a contest between Catholics and Protestants, as is popularly supposed. Nor were they contests between Scotland and England. Thomas Forster of Bamburgh was made General of the Jacobite forces south of the Tweed (despite having 'never seen an army in his life', according to the Lord Chancellor's wife, Lady Cowper) precisely because he could be seen to be both English and Protestant.

Many participants had mixed motives. Some Scots, for example, fought in the '15 because they opposed the political 1707 union of Scotland with England and wanted a return to a church ruled by bishops rather than Presbyterian elders. But the overriding impulse of most Jacobites was to uphold the traditions of legitimate, hereditary monarchy. They believed that the true line of succession to the throne had been broken when Mary, William and Anne had taken the Crown, even if it had been offered to them by Parliament. Many had sworn oaths of allegiance to James II as soldiers, lawyers and clergymen, and considered these sacred.

Even though they supported the man they believed to be their rightful king, those who fought on the Jacobite side were consistently called 'rebels' (and worse) by the de facto Hanoverian Government. After the risings failed, they were treated mercilessly – not as honourable prisoners of war.

The 1715 Rising began in Scotland on 6 September with the raising of the Jacobite standard on behalf of the Stuart King in exile, James III and VIII, at Braemar by John Erskine, 6th Earl of Mar. His followers went on to capture Perth, though not Edinburgh Castle. Until then, Mar's political allegiance had been equivocal to say the least: his nickname was Bobbing John. It is said that he only espoused the Jacobite cause when his attempts to win office under George I failed. Mar's precipitate action forced his Northumbrian co-conspirators, who had thus far managed to evade arrest as likely rebels, to come out for James III a little earlier than they had intended.

On 6 October, three of the main Northumbrian leaders – James Radcliffe, 3rd Earl of Derwentwater, his younger brother the Hon Charles Radcliffe (whose mother, Lady Mary Tudor, an illegitimate daughter of Charles II, was first cousin to James III), and Thomas Forster MP (who had estates at Bamburgh and Adderstone) – mustered their men at Waterfalls Hill, near Greenriggs. This moor between Ridsdale and Sweethope Lough – now marred by a massive wind farm – was a convenient meeting-place in the middle of the county for local gentry with Jacobite sympathies.

From Greenriggs they rode across Plainfield Moor to Rothbury, where they met more of the Northumbrian gentry. After a night at the Three Half-Moons Inn (now demolished), with supporters lodged in other places in the town, they rode into Warkworth with 500 men in arms and 60 armed horsemen. William, 4th Baron Widdrington, and his brothers Charles and Peregrine, all sons of a former Governor of Berwick, joined them on 8 October at Lesbury Common, close to Alnmouth, with about 30 horsemen and horses. On the same day, a group of 40 disaffected Berwickshire gentry with servants (who became known as the Merse Troop) rode into Coldstream to proclaim James VIII King of Scots in the Market Square. These included George Hume of Wedderburn, near Duns, his brother Francis Hume of Quixwood and George Hume of Whitfield. They crossed the River Tweed at the old fording-place and moved on to Lesbury.

That evening, Lord Derwentwater and 40 followers are said to have dined together in the Masons Arms, Warkworth. On Sunday, 9 October, they held a service at nearby St Lawrence Church, offering prayers for King James III and the exiled royal family. The vicar, William Ions, refused to conduct the service; instead, he rode to Newcastle to warn the authorities. General Thomas Forster, disguised as a herald and aided by a trumpeter called James Ossington, then raised the Stuart standard and publicly proclaimed James III at the Market-Place Cross. On 10 October (the day the Erringtons seized Lindisfarne Castle), news came that

Colonel Hotham's Regiment had arrived in Newcastle to oppose the 'rebels'. The Merse Troop left Lesbury for Felton to guard the bridge on the Great North Road, the third crossing-point of the River Coquet along with Rothbury and Warkworth.

How did Lindisfarne Castle feature in the 1715 Jacobite Rising?

Lindisfarne Castle, built in the 16th century, was of obvious strategic significance in any campaign, since it guarded the harbour at Holy Island. Neighbouring Bamburgh Castle was much bigger, but of no military value: while Thomas Forster strides its battlements in the Tale, in reality it had been in ruins since 1464, after being pounded into submission during the Wars of the Roses. Lindisfarne, with cannon and a garrison, was a danger to any invading force intending to land from the sea in that area or, if occupied by an enemy, a very useful aid to them. This was why it had been garrisoned in the Civil War by Parliamentarians. In 1715 it cannot have looked much like the castle romantically restored in 1901 by Sir Edwin Lutyens for Edward Hudson, founder of Country Life magazine. But at the time of the Rising, even as a small fort it was a prize worth taking.

Who were the Erringtons, in real life?

Lancelot Errington was owner and master of the brigantine Mary of Newcastle. A contemporary report claims that he had 'for several years been a common smuggler' on the coasts of North-East England and South-East Scotland. He had sailed from the Tyne a day or two after the first Jacobite muster at Greenriggs. It was suspected that the Mary was carrying stores for the Jacobite forces at Wooler, where a combined army of English and Scots insurgents did meet on 20 October. The ship was supposedly laden with salt destined for Norway, but Customs officers found it was carrying contraband brandy (which has a key role to play in Wilson's Tale). They seized this while the Erringtons were being dealt with by the soldiers, helped by volunteer townsmen from Berwick. A fierce dispute followed, over which of these men deserved the reward of half the illegal goods – and what their share should be when the

Crown's right to the other half was waived by George I, delighted at the prompt recapture of the castle.

Wilson rather plays down Lancelot Errington's very respectable family pedigree, linked to the Erringtons of West Denton, Newcastle. Whether Lancelot was related to Thomas Errington, called the 'Chief' of Beaufront, near Corbridge, is impossible to determine. Wilson implies this when he makes Lancelot claim that he had landed at Shields and travelled inland on the Jacobite king's business, visiting Beaufront and meeting with prominent men like Lord Derwentwater (whose seat at Dilston can be seen from Beaufront), Charles Radcliffe, Thomas Forster and representatives of the Shaftos, Swinburnes, Charltons, Hodgsons, Sandersons and other prominent Northumbrian Jacobite families. Wilson's historical and topographical references are correct, and such a meeting might well have taken place. In the Tale, fiction goes hand in hand with reality. Thomas Errington (not William) joined the Rising and, after its failure, was eventually pardoned and appointed northern agent for the confiscated Derwentwater estates. These were vast, stretching from Langley in the south to Alston Moor and Castlerigg in Cumberland to the west and as far north as Scremerston, near Berwick – where Cocklawburn Beach is still owned by Greenwich Hospital, to which all these estates were transferred by the Crown in 1735.

Wilson is right in naming Lancelot Errington's nephew as Mark but does not mention that his father, Francis Errington, owned Monks House – an ancient, sprawling property between Seahouses and Bamburgh. Mark lived and farmed there and was 26 years old at the time of the Rising. The romantic sub-plot of Mark's attachment to Sally Beadnell, and his subsequent marriage to her, is a fictional embellishment. The real Mark married a woman called Margaret. After his death she wrote a letter, appealing for relief from Lord Crewe's Charity, in which she mentioned that a pew her husband had given to Bamburgh Church had been sold without legal authority. This episode casts a different light on the fictional Mark

Errington, whom Wilson places lower down the social scale and characterises as piratical rather than pious.

The Erringtons' actions on 10 October 1715 seem to have been part of a plan in which James III was to land with supporters and French troops at the harbour on Holy Island, with the Northumbrian Jacobites joining him there or on the adjacent mainland. Unfortunately, their efforts were totally unsupported: the intended landing-place was switched to Alnmouth too late for them to be informed. Two French warships, expected to be carrying arms, were not warned either. They arrived off Holy Island belatedly on 14 October, signalled the castle and looked in vain for the Jacobite flag. It had been taken down after Captain Thomas Phillips, Captain Fawcett and three unnamed half-pay officers had led 20 or 30 soldiers and about 50 volunteer citizens from Berwick, with arms from the town's storehouse, to recover the castle for the Government. They had captured the Erringtons, who had abandoned it and were trying to flee the island. The French ships sailed on to Scotland, taking with them the best chance of the Rising. James III himself, short of money and arms, eventually landed much further north – at Peterhead, beyond Aberdeen – on 22 December, just as the Rising was coming to an end.

The Erringtons were, indeed, imprisoned in Berwick Gaol in Marygate after their capture. The present Town (or Guild) Hall stands on the same site but was rebuilt in its present form soon after the '15. Its cells are all on the upper floor, with none at ground-level as in the Tale, though Wilson describes them as having the same iron-grated windows that can be seen today.

That the Erringtons managed to escape before their trial, when they could expect to be executed if found guilty of 'treasonable' acts against the Hanoverian regime, confirms how resourceful they were. Most people in Berwick supported the Whig Government and the Protestant succession to the throne, but in the countryside around the town it was a very different story. There must have been some sympathy for the Jacobite cause among a minority of Berwickers: three of them, Thomas Bowring, Thomas Peach and Thomas Hunter, were later arrested and committed to gaol to await trial for aiding the escapees.

Lancelot's fame as the taker of Lindisfarne Castle brought him a Jacobite pension, paid via Lancelot Ord of Weetwood, who had escaped from prison and was now paymaster for the Jacobites abroad. But in 1718 Ord withdrew these payments, and Lancelot and 'Mr Charlton, a Northumberland gentleman' were described in a letter from a Captain John Ogilvie as being destitute and miserable. James III tried hard to support those refugees abroad who had lost all for his cause but did not have a bottomless purse and could not help every individual. Later the same year, Lancelot was going to be given the captaincy of a good ship to be presented to the king by a well-wisher; but nothing came of this. He returned to England quietly in 1720 and may have been the mariner who owned one-third of a house in the Pullen Market in Newcastle. In later accounts he is said to have owned the Salutation Inn at the head of the Flesh Market, frequented by Jacobite and Catholic gentlemen. The sentimental story that he died of grief on hearing of the failure of the 1745 Rising cannot be true: he was buried in St Nicholas' Churchyard on 22 December 1745, while the Battle of Culloden, the Jacobites' final (and only) defeat, took place nearly four months later on 16 April 1746.

And how did the '15 Rising end?

It never recaptured the enterprise and daring of the Lindisfarne raid. Lacking effective communications with Mar's forces to the north, and unaware of a rising of Lowland Jacobites in South-East Scotland, the Northumbrians were unclear what to do and meandered around, wasting valuable time. They rode to Alnwick and Morpeth, seeking more support with little success. They moved to Hexham, planned but abandoned a surprise attack on Newcastle, and finally combined with Scottish allies: Kenmure's Lowlanders at Rothbury and Borlum's Highlanders at Ednam, outside Kelso. The Jacobite army then marched through Cumbria into Lancashire – gaining little more support before the Battle of Preston on 14 November, where a combined force of some 1,500 Jacobites surrendered to the Hanoverian army. General Thomas Forster submitted to General Wills unconditionally without bargaining for the lives of his men, many of whom ended up on the gallows. On almost the same day, the indecisive Battle of Sheriffmuir took place in Scotland. Mar's forces had the upper hand but failed to pursue and rout the Duke of Argyle's Hanoverian army. The Rising then simply fizzled out.

Today the part played by Northumbrian insurgents in the '15 is still minimised or glossed over in history books. The Erringtons' capture of Lindisfarne Castle was one of the Rising's few successes. And the Erringtons themselves were among the lucky ones, since they escaped execution or retribution. Other Northumbrians were not so fortunate, dying in prison from disease or maltreatment, being beheaded like Lord Derwentwater, hanged, drawn and quartered like George Collingwood of Eslington, shot for desertion like Captain John Hunter of North Tyne, or transported to the Colonies into slavery, as happened with so many.

In Berwick, there is a permanent reminder of the '15: Berwick (or Ravensdowne) Barracks, the first purpose-built complex of its kind anywhere in Britain. It was built not only because the townsfolk were sick of having soldiers billeted on them in their own homes but in direct response to the threat that the Jacobite army had posed to the town – though in the event, Berwick was never attacked. The building work, between 1717 and 1721, was supervised by Captain Phillips, who captured the Erringtons. The Hanoverian royal coat of arms over the Main Gate makes a very clear statement of who intends to rule and maintain power in this region and in the whole country, to which Berwick was a gateway from Scotland.

Background by **John Nicholls**

Hume and the Governor of Berwick

Hume and the Governor of Berwick **retold**

Near the end of the 17th century, Lord Hume had an illegitimate son named Patrick. His mother was a Yetholm gypsy, and Patrick had the fiery temperament of both parents. A pretty girl to be loved or an Englishman killed, Patrick Hume was your man, caring nothing for bar, buttress, battlement, fire or water.

No one knows how Patrick and Isabel, daughter of the Mayor of Berwick, fell in love. What is known is that Patrick could not get to Isabel within the walls, or get her out. The best they could do was exchange endearments through a slit in the walls, a loophole.

Berwick was English. Its Mayor detested Scots Border raiders in general and Patrick Hume in particular. Into that young man's veins, he said, had been poured the raid-venom and love-poison of all gentlemen crooks that ever infested the Borders.

Detestation was mutual because up-river from Berwick was the Newmilne dam, preventing salmon swimming to the upper reaches. Patrick, a keen fisherman, threatened to demolish the dam and have both girl and salmon. The Mayor vowed he would get neither.

After one unsuccessful day's fishing, Patrick dozed on the bank before going to Isabel. But he overslept, leaping to his feet only when the moon came from behind a cloud, throwing its silver gleam across the river.

He cursed: "Late – three miles from love and honour. A loiterer in love is a laggard in war and shame on the Hume who is either."

He ran as fast as he could to look breathlessly through the loophole, heart pounding as Isabel's face appeared. He whispered: "Are you there at last, love? What kept you?"

"Ha!" she said. "You're the one who's late. I've been here an hour, sighing until the stones are hot. Where were you? With some gypsy? Now you ask what kept me? Ha! Good – for a Hume."

"The moon cheated me, hiding behind a cloud," said Patrick.

"And that threw love in the shade?" said Isabel. "I thought love kept its own time. What happens if there's a cloud on the night you said you'd get me free? I'd be back under the care of Captain Wallace."

Patrick snorted. "Ha! Good idea of your father's to offer you as a prize to the town governor. He knows he couldn't keep us apart unless he gave the captain an interest."

"You're right," said Isabel. "He's now got a man who'll guard town, Mayor and girl. What are you going to do?"

Before he could reply she went on, "And what I'm going to tell you now should sharpen your wits and strengthen your arm: Captain Wallace has been given a date to marry me."

"What?" Patrick shouted. "You're joking, Bell? When?"

"A week today," said Isabel. "But keep quiet: here he comes, blowing like a grampus."

Fat, boastful and throaty, Captain Wallace was, by his own account, a hero of Bothwell Bridge. He had not been there. But after a fourth bottle of wine with the Mayor he was in full flow as the pair came to look for Isabel.

"I told you she'd be here," Wallace told the Mayor. "Anything to do with war impresses women."

"But it's the outside of these walls she loves," said the Mayor, as they saw Isabel moving away from the loophole. "I don't like this, Captain. Aha! I see Patrick Hume. Be brave and drive your sword through the loophole. You might blind him."

"I like to fight fair," said the Captain, "man to man as we did on Bothwell Bridge." He lowered his voice: "But to please you, and get rid of a rival, I might as well kill him this way. Here goes."

Patrick saw the sword shoot through the slit in the wall. Handkerchief round hand, he grabbed the point and yanked. Captain Wallace, hero of Bothwell, yelled as his sword vanished.

Recovering, he said: "Don't run away, Mayor. I forget you weren't at Bothwell. But I think I've done for him. Patrick Hume, you say? Then he's as dead as my grandmother — and my fiancée and your dam are safe."

"Don't be so sure," said the Mayor. "That Hume's a devil. He might be badly wounded, but I wouldn't like to get in the way of the dying tiger. Let's get home."

Hearing them leave, Patrick came back to the loophole, hoping for Isabel. When she did not return, already locked in her room by her father, Patrick bent the Governor's sword double, cursed him and the Mayor, and set off home. At the moonlit Newmilne dam, an idea struck him.

"Got it! Where's the equal of the bastard Hume? Bell, if you only knew what I have in mind."

Next morning Patrick made a round of local Scottish landowners. Two days later, placards appeared in Berwick — announcing that at 10 o'clock the following Monday, Scots gentlemen would demolish Newmilne dam. The Mayor asked all townsmen to go with him and Captain Wallace to defend Berwick's property.

Berwickers at that time were prejudiced against Border Scots, and Patrick soon heard that Mayor and Governor would have strong support. Captain Wallace began drilling volunteers. His loud voice, proud bearing, bent back (self defence against the weight of his stomach) and martial strut impressed his troops and gave them confidence.

On that Monday the chronicle of the time noted: "Many hundred people on horse and foote were gathered together, considerably armed with swordes, pistoles, firelocks, blunderbuses, fowling pieces, bowes and arrows and other powerful ammunition to resist the ryot of the Scotch… away they marched to the Newmilne with Mr Mayor and the Governor, a verrie terrible man of war."

Patrick and his companions, hiding behind brushwood, watched and smiled as the small army went past. When it had gone they set off for Berwick, a town now without a guard.

At Newmilne there was no sign of Scots. Captain Wallace faced the wood from where attack was expected and called upon the cowards to come out.

"I told you I'd killed Patrick Hume," he bawled to the Mayor. "If I didn't, where is he? And the rest of the Border heroes? Ha, ha! The rascals must have been at Bothwell and felt the power of my arm."

As he started slashing tops off young firs to show how strong that arm was, Berwick's bells were heard, followed almost immediately by panting messengers: the Bastard Hume and followers had taken Isabel, and she seemed happy to go. But, the messengers said, Hume didn't have much of a start and could be caught if Wallace and his men took a shortcut.

The Mayor seized the idea, the armed Berwick townsmen shouted for action, and drums and fifes pealed. Captain Wallace did his best to strike a warlike pose and his 16 stones of beef walked as fast as alternating waves of fear, shame and spurious bravery would permit. Quickly, using the shortcut, the Berwickers caught up with Hume's men in a wood. There they were drinking wine provided by a laughing Isabel.

The Berwick men stopped short, a move thoroughly approved by Captain Wallace. But the Mayor strode towards the enemy. "Traitor!" he shouted to Hume. "Getting us to Newmilne so you could seize my daughter won't work. Hand her back."

Hume said: "You can have her if you can take her – or if she's willing to go."

Isabel came forward: "No. I love my father and the good citizens of Berwick. I don't want them hurt. If there's a fight, it should be only between Governor Wallace and Patrick Hume."

"Bravo!" shouted the Berwickers; and Isabel, delighted with her plan, hid a smile behind her shawl. All turned to look expectantly at Captain Wallace, but the hero of Bothwell Bridge was whispering frantically to the Mayor. Hume, sword in hand, was ready to fight.

"Come on, Captain," he called.

"Come forward!" shouted Isabel and the Berwickers.

Captain Wallace kept the Mayor between him and Hume. His voice trembled: "I'm the Governor of Berwick. As the King's servant I can't run the risk of losing authority by... by... engaging, I say, by committing myself in single combat like a knight errant. It's not dignified... eh... eh... I can't lower myself from the glory of Bothwell to a love brawl. But you're my men, eh? You're bound to fight when I tell you? Do your duty. Rescue her."

"We don't want her," the men called out. "The man that won't fight for the woman he loves deserves to lose her."

"Bravo, men!" cried Isabel, and Hume's followers rewarded her courage with a cheer. Berwickers caught their enthusiasm and were soon sharing their wine, all shouting: "Hurray for Hume!"

The Mayor realised that both sides now supported Isabel and her partner. "Hume," he said, "come here. And you, Isabel."

She threw her arms round her father's neck as the men cheered and shouted. "I'm sorry," she said, "but you can see I've made the right choice. One's a coward, the other a brave young man."

"I forgive you, Bell," said the Mayor, placing her hand in Hume's. "Come on, Captain, forgive her too and we can all be friends."

He looked round for the Captain. So did everyone else. But the hero was gone. He'd mounted a horse, as thin as he was fat, and was propelling her to Berwick with sword whacks on the unfortunate beast's protruding ribs. The sight of the rapidly receding pair, swollen body on thin horse, and fearful flight after a day of boasting, brought a roar of laughter. Captain Wallace only whacked harder and rode on, never stopping until he reached Berwick.

"He'd mounted a horse, as thin as he was fat..." An original illustration from Wilson's Tales of the Borders.

Patrick and Isabel married, their health drunk by Berwickers. But his scheme to get the girl, although admired for its cunning, was not noted in town council records. These read simply: "An expedition was made to Newmilne dam where they braived the Scots to come and fecht. But the cowardes never appeared."

Retold by **Fordyce Maxwell**

Background to *Hume and the Governor of Berwick*

The tale of Hume and the Governor of Berwick is an interesting conundrum for the historian.

At face value it is a simple tale of star-crossed lovers: Patrick, an illegitimate son of a "Lord Hume of the latter part of the 17th century" and Isabella, the daughter of the (unnamed) Mayor of Berwick. Patrick and the Mayor are not on speaking terms owing to Hume's threat to dismantle the weir at New Mills on the River Whiteadder, just upstream of Canty's Bridge. Throw into this the Governor of Berwick, one Captain Wallace, to whom Isabella's hand in marriage is promised by Mr Mayor, and the scene is set for a good old-fashioned tussle of wills.

But did any of it actually happen? And did Wilson intend his Tale to be more than a simple love story?

The first challenge is placing the story in time. The only clue we have is Captain Wallace's bragging in Falstaffian manner about his heroics on the battlefield. He repeatedly references Bothwell as the scene of his greatest hour, this being the Battle of Bothwell Bridge of 1679. If Captain Wallace had been at Bothwell and was now a veteran, that might place the story at the end of the 17th century. However there is no known Governor of Berwick by the name Wallace in the 17th century.

Until 1850, the military in Berwick was controlled by a Governor. Although Berwick had been in English hands since 1482, there was always a tension until the Union of the Crowns in 1603 — and then afterwards due to the English Civil Wars and, later, the Jacobite risings. The town was patrolled and the gates closed every night until the end of the Napoleonic Wars in 1815. The Guild of Freemen was the body of burgesses that controlled all civilian aspects of life in Berwick. From their number they elected a Mayor who had final say on all things and could even pass a sentence of death in the court over which he presided until 1835. Together, the military and civilian rubbed along, usually each with a grudging respect for the other.

The lovers' meeting place is a cannon loop-hole in the defensive walls of Berwick, through which they talk of their love and plot to elope. This sounds at odds with the presumed late 17th century timeframe. The Elizabethan walls were built by 1570 but have no simple loop-holes. The meeting place is therefore likely to have been one of the medieval towers on the north stretch of walls near the Bell Tower — probably Broadstairhead Tower, which stood on the site of Holy Trinity School. It is known that these walls were still in use in 1640 despite the Elizabethan 'replacement' and so may well have still been patrolled in the 1680s; a map of 1682 shows the old wall in profile, suggesting this was important information to convey. The loop-hole is also surely an allusion to Ovid's tale of Pyramus and Thisbe, the forbidden lovers who converse through a crack in a wall made famous by Shakespeare's Mechanicals in *A Midsummer Night's Dream*.

What of the contentious New Mills dam-dike, to which the Mayor and Wallace are lured? New Mills was a complex of different industries owned by the Freemen, the mills themselves, a number of small quarries and the nearby salmon fisheries by the mill and a little further downstream at Canty's Bridge. A weir—the "dam-dike" of Wilson's tale—channelling water to the mill race still exists, along with other remains.

This would undoubtedly have prevented fish from migrating upstream. Around this time, modern angling was becoming popular — Izaak Walton published his famous work *The Compleat Angler* in 1652 — and one can see that the landed gentry would have objected to the building of a weir. This was possibly constructed in 1663 when the 'new' mill was built to replace an earlier one.

Intriguingly, Frederick Sheldon in his *History of Berwick-upon-Tweed* (1849) relates a dispute over the 'dam of the Newe Milne' between Lord Hume and the Guild of Freemen of Berwick. Sheldon was in many ways similar to John Mackay Wilson. He too was interested in the Border Ballads, writing a *Minstrelsy Of The English Border* in response to Walter Scott's earlier work. And, like Wilson, he died very young (aged 34) having lived in poverty all his life. But Sheldon's work cannot be trusted for its accuracy: his romanticised account of Berwick's past is written to appeal to his reader's imagination. As it was written after Wilson published his Tale, one would not be surprised if Sheldon had incorporated Wilson's story into his work.

But in fact, Sheldon seems to have plagiarised almost word for word an episode in a book by John Mason entitled *THE BORDER TOUR Throughout THE MOST IMPORTANT AND INTERESTING PLACES IN THE COUNTIES OF NORTHUMBERLAND, BERWICK, ROXBURGH, and SELKIRK*. This work was published in 1826, importantly before Wilson wrote his story.

This is the primary inspiration for Wilson's tale. It is specific, in that the events took place on 10th May 1683, and describes how the tenant at New Mills sends word to Berwick that, at 10 o'clock that morning, Lord Hume and other 'Scotch neighbours' and their tenants were to turn up at the mill to destroy the dam. A posse of some 300 men, some ex-soldiers, is hastily mustered to march with the Mayor on the Scots and defend the Liberties of Berwick. They arrive on time and hang about for a few hours before returning to Berwick, the Scots threat having never materialised.

In this account, Captain Wallace is referred to as being the Governor of Berwick. As it is known he was not Governor (in 1683, that honour would have belonged to Henry Cavendish, 2nd Duke of Newcastle-upon-Tyne) he may have been Deputy Governor.

But he did exist. In 1680, a dispute arose in Berwick when Charles Jackson, the youngest son of Stephen Jackson, a Freeman, challenged the rules on admittance to the Guild. This led to the surrender of the 1604 Royal Charter to Charles II. One of the people entrusted with the presentation of the Charter to the king was one Captain James Wallace.

Interestingly, in Mason's version of the New Mills dispute, "Charles Jackson and William Couttie, in the time the town's people were out, went to the bell tower and by way of derision, rung the alarum bell there, as if it had beene a great invasion there to be made." And William Couttie is recorded in 1684 as being the master gunner of the garrison!

So it would appear that this tale is based on, and embellishes, a true story. A device that George MacDonald Fraser uses in his 'historic' Flashman novels is to take a piece of known history (especially when not all the facts are known) and place his anti-hero among the protagonists. In much the same way, Wilson takes entire passages from Mason's story, only occasionally rewording them to suit his narrative, and adds other characters.

For instance, Mason suggests the alarm bell was rung as the Mayor, Wallace and company returned to Berwick. Wilson adds the extra dimension of a love story, and the alarm bell summons the Berwickers back when the deception is discovered.

So far, so good. But several interesting coincidences suggest that Wilson's tale might also be an allegory in support of Presbyterianism.

The young Patrick Hume is probably fictitious. There was a George Hume, Earl of Dunbar who resided in a large palace built on the site of Berwick Castle; but he died in 1611 without any male issue. Wilson is probably drawing inspiration from Sir Patrick Hume, 1st Baronet and later Lord Polwarth. He was born in 1641 and was a staunch defender of the Presbyterian Covenanters. In 1683, when our Tale can be supposed to be set, he was in hiding and attempting to escape to the Continent, having been accused of complicity in the Rye House Plot, an attempt to assassinate Charles II. A staunch defender of Scottish Presbyterianism, in 1685 he took part in the failed Argyll Expedition in support of the Monmouth Rebellion to oust James VII/II. Escaping, this time to Utrecht, in what must be a coincidence, he went under the name 'Dr Wallace'. He returned when William of Orange swept to power in 1688, had his lands restored, and died in Berwick in 1702.

Since the 18th century the bastard has been seen as a free spirit challenging the establishment. Wilson was raised in the Presbyterian tradition and may have seen himself as the hero Patrick Hume, a personification of the underdog Covenanters. Is it any coincidence that Hume's rival for the hand of Isabella is a veteran of the Battle of Bothwell Bridge, at which a rebellion of Scottish Presbyterian Covenanters was finally put down by Government troops? Which side Wallace fought for we are not told, but logically he would have been on the 'English' Government side.

The Mayor of Berwick in 1683 was George Watson. Whether he had a daughter is not known. But Isabella surely represents the freedom of choice that the Covenanters desired. She is a reference to another romantic heroine, another rebel from Berwick's turbulent times – Isabella, Countess of Buchan, who was imprisoned in a cage in Berwick Castle in 1306. Indeed, Wilson's Isabella tells young Patrick that since she had been promised to Wallace, she is "more firmly caged than ever was the old countess".

So: simple love story or allegorical story of a people's fight for religious freedom? You decide.

Background by **Jim Herbert**

Further reference

Sheldon's History
https://books.google.co.uk/books/about/History_of_Berwick_upon_Tweed.html?id=oQwNAAAAYAAJ&redir_esc=y

Mason's History
https://books.google.co.uk/books?id=DbIxAQAAIAAJ&source=gbs_slider_cls_metadata_7_mylibrary

Reference to Wallace and Jackson (from Scott's *History of Berwick* 1888)
http://www.electricscotland.com/history/berwick/chapter12.htm

The contributors

ANDREW AYRE, a resident of Tweedmouth, founded the Wilson's Tales Project in 2013 to celebrate and revive interest in Wilson's Tales and some of the local stories and heritage embedded in them.

He first became aware of the Tales as a child, when the title was given to someone to perform as a New Year charade. Now an accountant by profession, he has maintained a keen interest in history, literature and local events. He is currently reading his way through the Tales and researching for future events, publications and talks.

www.wilsonstales.co.uk

MICHAEL A FENTY is a retired GP living in Coldingham. He has been writing for many years – initially articles for medical magazines and later, after retirement, drama.

Michael's play *The Resurrection Man* – based on the letters and trial documents of local doctor George Laurie, tried in 1820 for grave robbing – was performed by the New Strides Theatre Company; and last year he contributed four short plays to a dramatised walk in the Lammermuirs – *The Footsteps of Flodden*.

The Royal Raid was his first dramatisation of a Wilson's Tale. His next, *The Monomaniac*, was performed at Paxton House in 2014.

Michael's blog *Gangril Days* is at **http://gangrildays.blogspot.co.uk/**

JOE LANG began his writing career as a journalist, playwright and advertising copywriter. He started a London-based communications consultancy business, which he ran for 30 years before moving to Berwick and rediscovering the joys of freelance life.

joe@kaineslang.com

MARY KENNY is a storyteller living in Innerleithen. Her repertoire of tales is broad and deep, but includes a special love for the stories and ballads of the Borderlands.

A visual artist for 35 years, with work in public and private collections at home and abroad, Mary has a workshop in the grounds of Traquair House. She also sings with Borders-based a cappella group The Fisher Lassies.

"As an oral storyteller," she says, "the challenge of working with this extraordinary, encyclopaedic collection of tales is to adapt what can be a flowery and outmoded style of written language, and re-interpret the story sensitively for a new audience".

www.marykenny.co.uk

JIM HERBERT has lived in Berwick for 37 years and worked in the heritage industry for the past 17. He loves the history of Berwick-upon-Tweed, Northumberland and the Borders. As well as being a historian he is a designer, actor, technician and siege engineer!

Jim runs Berwick Time Lines, a service offering, among other things, regular tours and talks. He writes a regular Berwick Time Lines blog. Dedicated to Berwick's rich history, he researches stories of the town, its people and buildings, often discovering new truths about the past. He also loves prog rock and playing pool.

For more information about services and Jim's blog, visit www.berwicktimelines.com and www.berwicktimelines.tumblr.com

JOHN NICHOLLS MBE lives in Hume, Berwickshire. Educated at Newcastle Royal Grammar School and at University College Oxford, he went on to become an English teacher, Head of English and Deputy Headmaster. In 1990 he left teaching and, with his wife, Elizabeth, opened a guesthouse, Treetops, in East Ord, near Berwick. In 1995, they won Tourism's Oscar from the English Tourist Board as the best B&B in England. In 2005, John was made an MBE 'for services to the Tourist Industry and to the community in Northumberland'. Before retirement, he was Registrar at Coldstream. He is Chairman and Journal Editor of The Fifteen (The Northumbrian Jacobite Society) and a trustee of The Hume Castle Preservation Trust.

www.northumbrianjacobites.org.uk

FORDYCE MAXWELL, oldest of a family of nine from Cramond Hill Farm, Cornhill on Tweed, was educated at Berwick Grammar School and Harper Adams Agricultural College. He has been a journalist since 1967. Much of that time was with *The Scotsman* as agricultural and rural affairs editor, columnist, diarist, Parliamentary sketch writer, feature writer, leader writer and book reviewer. He has freelanced for many other newspapers and magazines and continues to do so, including as Halidon in the Tweeddale Press. He has received the MBE for services to journalism and the Scottish Newspaper Editors' award for lifetime achievement.

DAVID AYRE has wanted to dramatise Scotland's past from an early age. He first studied the Flodden tale of *The Faithful Wife* as part of his sixth-form drama project and told the tale in his own words at The Scottish Storytelling Pub, situated where the Flodden wall used to be. He subsequently worked as a volunteer reporter to the Flodden 500 project and an intern with the Wilson's Tales Project. He then spent a season as a windsurfing instructor and comedian/storyteller. He now plays a fudgemaker from the 1830s in one of Edinburgh's tourist attractions on the Royal Mile.

www.Ayremythoughts.wordpress.com

NICK JONES recently moved to Northumberland after years milling organic stoneground flour and organising arts projects in Cumbria. He writes short stories and plays, the most recent inspired by Northumbrian culture, history, tourism, watermills, compost heaps, oceanic plastic, and rubbish in general.

nicolasjbjones@gmail.com and www.jonesnick@wordpress.com